The College Admission

Life Hacks for the process from Application to Graduation

Dr. Christopher Salute

The College Admission – College Life Hacks from Application to Graduation

Copyright © 2021 by Dr. Christopher Salute

All rights reserved

Published by Red Penguin Books

Bellerose Village, New York

Library of Congress Control Number: 2022911733

ISBN

Print 978-1-63777-217-1

Digital 978-1-63777-218-8

This is a work of fiction, any similarity to anyone living or dead or companies or institutes is purely coincidental.

No part of this book may be reproduced in any form or by any electronic or mechanical means, including information storage and retrieval systems, without written permission from the author, except for the use of brief quotations in a book review.

I would like to thank my family and friends who have had to endure me discussing my dream of finishing this book for 3+ years. Mom and Dad have always been supportive of what I do. So, thank you. A special thank you to Elizabeth Litfin. Through her love and friendship, I have found a way to finish this first book. Timarie… I also look to you as my benchmark. Thank you for keeping me on my game in finishing this book.

A special recognition to Dr. Rob Valli for his support as well as his foreward. To my colleagues and friends (including former students) who have contributed, I so much appreciate your input and support.
To my publisher, Stephanie Larkin, for believing in me enough to green light this and my next book… Thank you.
Lastly, to my followers, readers, etc. who are buying this book… thank you for keeping print alive!

CONTENTS

Foreword	vii
Let's Get our Shoes Dirty	xv
1. THE MOST IMPORTANT DECISION OF YOUR LIFE	1
From the Experts	10
Professor's Pro Tip	10
2. YOU CAN'T HAVE YOUR CAKE AND EAT IT, TOO	15
From the Experts	22
Professor's Pro Tip	23
3. MENTORSHIP, NETWORKING, AND SOCIAL NETWORKING	27
From the Experts	36
Professor's Pro Tip	37
4. SELECTING YOUR CAREER THEN YOUR MAJOR	43
From the Experts	50
Professor's Pro Tip	51
5. THE INTERNSHIP PARADIGM	55
Professor's Pro Tip	63
From the Experts	63
Professor's Pro Tip	64
Worksheet	64
6. MINDFULNESS AND DIET	67
Professor's Pro Tip	76
Statistics	77
7. ACADEMICS	79
From the Experts	86
Professor's Pro Tips	87
8. OUTSIDE OF THE CLASSROOM	93
Professor's Pro Tips	101
From the Experts	102
Worksheet	102
Skill:	103

9. PRESENTATIONS AND PAPERS	105
Professor's Pro Tip	115
From the Experts	116
10. THE INTERVIEW	121
Professor's Pro Tip	129
From the Experts	130
Afterword	133
About the Author	135

FOREWORD

"Universities have become what the urban industrial districts once were. The modern American campus is anything but an ivory tower. It is a crossroads of civilization—a place where bright people from all over the world converge, a place to find teachers and mentors, make contacts, where many disciplines and trades intersect. The campus, in short, is the new natural locus of public/private engagement—a gigantic Ellis Island through which corporate executives pass."
(Paul Magelli, Academic Thought Leader & Pioneer, 2008)

In his farewell address, President Dwight D. Eisenhower famously warned U.S. citizens about the "military–industrial complex." The expression "military–industrial complex" (MIC) describes the relationship between a nation's military and the defense industry that supplies it, seen together as a vested interest which influences public policy. A driving factor behind the relationship between the military and the defense-minded corporations is that both sides benefit—one side from obtaining war weapons, and the other from being paid to supply them.

A thirty year 'arms race' in higher education has led to what some might regard as the emergence of the "Academic-industrial complex."

For the college-bound high school student this complex labyrinth presents formidable challenges to vetting, identifying and choosing an optimal path towards forging passions and career-readiness. For parents/guardians, the landscape of academia might evoke head-scratching as to the nature of academia which might better resemble *'The Last Bastian of the Soviet system'*, in turn, making the prospect of the college journey bewildering.

A new paradigm of higher education has arrived. Today's dynamic market drivers are challenging academia in unprecedented ways. The decade ahead in higher education requires us to rethink the concept of college. In the book, <u>The College Admission: College Life Hacks from Application to Graduation,</u> academic strategist Dr. Chris Salute offers a beacon into the nuances of managing and optimizing the college journey.

Salute's academic research and career trajectory offer traction and credibility at a time when the landscape of academia is shifting at warp speed, where vital themes for transforming the college experience is the new imperative. Recognizing the challenges of modern-day education is one thing, offering valued input and tangible solutions to those college bound are much more difficult. Yet, Salute manages to speak directly to GenZ in the language of its generation. His scholarly pursuit and operational management experience offers an articulation that is both understandable and compelling to not only the young, but also lifetime learners.

Effectively navigating through massive disruption confronting academia today necessitates an acute sensitivity to the ethos of GenZ and a tacit awareness of college-sown skills that meet market demands. At minimum, universities are expected to diagnose problems, leverage collaborations and apply solutions. However, ever increasing societal expectations demand accelerated analysis and relevant concepts towards impact and influence. Salute incorporates the ideology of the *people, place and purpose* of higher education today. He cleverly harnesses relevant research at the conclusion of every Chapter that serves to propel critical thinking and cutting-edge practices that impact the spectrum of student experience.

Dr. Salute's academic research is cross-disciplinary, before it was fashionable—serving as an intellectual nexus blending *third stream initiatives* i.e., the importance of taking the analysis and concepts from the classroom and applying them in a meaningful way that enhances learning and a sense of building the student's future worthiness in the eyes of society and industry.

The essence of <u>The College Admission</u> is to provide a thematic spade for spearheading a collegiate pathway where a student's relevance, reach and respect are priorities. This book offers a window into the unique qualities and implications of the academic support system for instructional design, bridging theory and practice within the overarching themes of Career-readiness-Creativity-Communication. As a Servant Leader, Salute's strategic vision engenders positive outputs that are core to *learning, living, and well-being!*

There are opportunities and threats along the road to graduation: culture-recognition, social ecosystems and robust academic programs that impact one's employability. The changing values of Gen 'Y' and 'Z', combined with Salute's progressive ethos, offer genuine synergies to catapult a university's value proposition for students, well beyond the province of one's college-of-choice. Unleashing the student's entrepreneurial spirit requires an author who is a proactive listener, a rare 'student of the academia,' whose hybrid skills and experience reflect a process-oriented approach to achieving student 'buy-in.'

First, and foremost, Salute is a 'team-player.' He approaches the reader with 'hat-in-hand,' seeking first to understand the students faculty and stakeholders who together make up the State of the Academic Industrial Complex and…its peculiar culture.

Salute is a collaborator whose writings consistently illuminate: the ability to leverage complementary resources that enhance core competencies and a penchant for educating tomorrow's leaders. Salute is preoccupied with the notion: personal growth through agility. The book's concepts inspire self-efficacy and the importance of student-confidence. Salute possesses an acute sense of propriety for honoring institutional intent and student success. His transparent writing style is based on the law of 'attraction' rather than 'promotion:' put 'people first' and the results will follow. Ultimately, Salute is an enabler in the most positive sense of the word.

What excites me most about The College Admission is that the book offers a nexus for blending third-stream initiatives via innovation, experiential learning, and entrepreneurship-bridging disciplines into worthy skills that catapult student experience.

At a time when differentiation in higher education has become increasingly challenging, Salute builds upon the Academy's existing attributes while embracing complex market-drivers, guiding personal and professional development at a time of intensified focus.

Technology-based disruption, changing roles of multinational corporations, public policy- making and the growth of new enterprise require that higher education adapt. The College Admission inevitably strives to inspire students to embrace change and squelch fears. The reader is left with clearly articulated goals, strategic pathways that support goals, a timeline, and a means of measuring progress… answering the question, 'How can a student better optimize the college experience?'

A key element for advancing the student experience from 'application to graduation' is the ability to inspire curiosity, critical to securing optimal opportunities. Salute implies that every action taken impacts each student in a different way and requires the subtle orchestration of multiple constituents and activities.

The following examples represent some strategic tactics for enhancing student experience.
- Take a thematic approach: identify areas of potential growth in

mindset by selecting curriculum aimed at entrepreneurial and professional development
- Learn the subtle nuances of university culture that most resonate
- Emphasis on translational skills that meet today's market demands
- Maintain mechanisms for interdisciplinary sharing and networking
- Stress student-efficacy via engaged learning
- Seek asymmetrical alliances with students possessing complementary skills
- Attend *Thought Leadership Forums* designed to pique curiosity
- Increase 'touch-points' with mentors and advisors focusing on critical thinking and solutions
- Identify universities that seek outcomes for the sake of society

A convergence of four economic drivers have changed the landscape for student protocol and university competitiveness:
- <u>GLOBALIZATION</u> – the integration of national economies into global economy is making the *'world flat'* for the transformation of ideas
- <u>KNOWLEDGE</u> – the service sector has eclipsed agriculture and manufacturing as the leading industry domain; seventy percent of the workers in developed economies are information workers, making human capital a key asset class
- <u>CREATIVITY</u> – the Internet has created an information and borderless super-highway, making accessibility chiefly indifferent to locality
- <u>ENTREPRENEURSHIP & SUSTAINABILITY</u> - Technology will be the rebirth of Liberal Arts

Human behavior is a manifestation of feelings. Before stating, "*Here's what we want to do*," it is imperative to understand the core values that shape a student's entrepreneurial mindset. *How* do we nurture student development and transformation? What is the '*Heart & Soul*' of the student's core values? The answer may be ... '*Entrepreneurial Thinking*' impacting and influencing humanity ... the engine of a student's mindset is personal growth.

Salute suggests key themes for outlining critical priorities that chart a course that embraces the ideals of the Liberal Arts while being anchored in the practical world of step-by-step execution. A fundamental principle of *'inclusion'* is that more can be accomplished through professional development and experiential learning. Leveraging university's existing academic themes, while honing-in on relevance (i.e., application) offers a compelling attribute to students seeking a personal brand that differentiates, making the student investable in the eyes of future employers. One way is through student-consultancies that attract public/private partners and alumni by serving as an *'external arm of business intelligence'*-harnessing *all-important professional contacts* while engaging the community at large. These mentors lend tacit knowledge and social networks.

Salute implies that *Design Thinking* resides where the *'Ivory Tower and Main Street' converge.* The importance of students pursuing third-stream initiatives is the emphasis on transforming research into practicum. Many drivers underscore the increasing challenges of commercializing university ideas. Salute suggests that student ambition, combined with modern skills, can impact regional economic development.

Multiple levels of skill attainment might include, leveraging 'Personal Initiatives:'
- Coordinating a personal roadmap for driving a 'growth mindset' Enterprise Creation
  - Open Innovation Practices
  - Digital Learning Modules
  - Professional Development
  - Well-Being
  - Designed 'touch-points'
  - Functioning under the umbrella of a <u>Regenerative Economy</u>

Salute posits a fundamental core value that includes helping students get a *'job,'* i.e., *building their own investability.* Employing a thematic-centric/applied-oriented, *plan of study* challenges a student to identify a *problem,* take-*action* and show *results* through *collaborative solutions.* At the core is heightened student-efficacy.

The new imperative in Leadership Education is ***agility***, embracing disruption under interwoven design-principles:
- Enterprise Engagement
- Interdisciplinary Collaboration
- Purpose-driven Ideology
- Professional Certification

Trending pedagogy highlights the *Higher Science of Human and Institutional Excellence* by complementing the student's academic focus with a blend of market-driven personal and professional development. Thus, enriching the student while inspiring others.

Salute possesses the integration of a visionary who has experience navigating complex market drivers, the skill to harness collective ambition, and the ability to inspire an entrepreneurial spirit among faculty, staff, student, and public/private partners alike. The difference is that he genuinely puts students first! Salute's frontline academic experience has prepared him to act in a dynamic capacity, where student-efficacy is at a premium. His career trajectory spans a Ph.D. in Psychology, new venture formation, digital media, as well as academic administration. All of this offers a unique arsenal of hybrid skills which is transformed in his teachings. Salute's mantra is 'build student-confidence' through first-hand experience, emphasizing the imperative of building a student's 'investability' via industry engagement. Complementing theoretical concepts from the classroom with project-based problem-solving fosters compelling stories to articulate when seeking differentiation in the interview process. Throughout his professional and academic career, Salute has managed projects from concept to fruition. This operating experience is underpinned by a *vision-to-action-skill-set,* transforming ideas into measurable and meaningful impact—an ability to initiate and execute new programs and processes to navigate through the growing challenges of differentiation in business education. In doing so, he has gained an expansive global network to leverage today's convergence of technology, globalization and connectivity. Salute possesses a proclivity for advancing public/private partnership on a worldwide platform. Stewarding the coordination of knowledge and practice across a broad spectrum of emerging global leadership topics plays to his diverse strengths. In this vein, Salute has a successful record of building revenue-generating, cutting-edge academic programs, with a heightened sensitivity for the student experience with the end goal in mind: personal growth and the agility to embrace change for sustainable professional engagement.

In <u>The College Admission: College Life Hacks from Application to Graduation</u>, Dr. Salute underscores unlocking student potential via the University's entrepreneurial ecosystem, where tacit understanding of the Academy's culture climate and student are front and center at a premium.

Carpe diem!

Dr. Robert Valli, Former University President

Cambridge University

LET'S GET OUR SHOES DIRTY

Yo, it's me... Ya boy. Okay, I know we don't know each other, but we're about to get really acquainted. My name is Christopher, and I love making mistakes. Why? Because then I get to teach others how to do things right. I am the Dean of a Private University, a small business owner and entrepreneur four times over, a master networker, and I love to hang out with and teach young people. I have a dog named Joker, and I live in Las Vegas, Nevada...but I grew up in New York... home of the helicopter parent and high-strung teenager. I'm here to tell you a few things. You're going to like some of them. Some of them you won't agree with. And that's cool. But this book is all about setting yourself up for success in college and afterward.

Who are you? You're age 15-20 (or the parent of) and you're struggling to figure out who you are. Hey, it's all good. I am, too. Want to know the best part about life? Tomorrow we can make a decision that will change who we are going forward. Don't say "I always do that." Start saying "I always did that." Now say, "Here's what I am going to do." We start this process now.

Life is meant to be more than fast food, Tinder swipes, and video games. Life is meant to be so enjoyable and wonderful that when we do those things, we do them with a super clear head and lots of resources. You cool with that? Let's jump in...

When I was around 30 years old and finishing my Ph.D., my mother asked me to sit down with my little cousin and talk him into going to a four-year traditional academic institution. She said that there was a possibility that he'd go into the military or potentially a trade school, maybe both. How horrid, right? "Speak some sense into him," she said.

"But, why?" I asked.

"Because you went through a lot of school and look how you turned out."

First of all, my life is a challenge just like everyone else's is. There are times in which I wish I could give back the degrees I have in exchange for the absurd amount of money I spent on them. But, yes, I am glad to be an MBA and a Doctor. Still, further education (or, more specifically, university education) is not for everyone. People in the trades make a ton of money, especially in New York, as do people who have an entrepreneurial spirit and start a successful dry cleaning company. Not everyone has to go the traditional route of college or university.

However, it is the right path for some. So, how do you choose?

This is the conversation that consistently brings me the most phone calls from friends, the most business, and the most frustration.

There are too many factors to consider when looking at every type of college, university, the military, the workforce, trade school, and all of the infinite other possibilities you could consider.

>Should you be looking for a four-year institution?
>Two-year Associates?
>For-profit?
>Non-profit?
>Trade school?
>Online certification?
>Military training?
>Large?
>Small?

Urban?
Suburban?

Did you know the reason we don't have every possible food option at a grocery store? It's because too many boxes of cereal will paralyze us! When we can't make a decision, we don't. We stop. **So stop doing that. Don't get paralyzed.**

What you need to do is narrow your search by understanding yourself.

"Seriously? Understand myself? Just like that... understand myself."

Yes... just like that.

I mean...not JUST like that. But seriously. START understanding yourself. (We'll get into self-reflection throughout this book.)
As you're understanding yourself, start the search. You know, because your brain says so, you can delete half of those choices off the list. Maybe even two-thirds.
Keep that smaller list, now start to research. Watch videos; ask friends who have experienced what you're looking for. VISIT some spots close and far from home. Do it on a budget if you have to and just visit one. You'll understand pretty quickly if you like small schools when you visit Siena College (my alma mater) versus a large school like Stony Brook University (the largest state university on Long Island where I grew up).
The rest... is up to your heart.
So, you pick a spot, your favorite spot. Front porch? Treehouse? Deli? Beach? Next to the dumpster in your high school? I don't care.

Put.
Down.
Your.
Damn.
Phone.
(Keep it there.)

And think. Think about all of the choices you have left. Which have you visited and loved? Which can you actually see yourself in? Start narrowing them all down. Where do the mid-sized schools fit? Secular? Non-secular? Do you want fast food options on campus or cute cafes in a college town? Do you want diversity? Folks living on campus (this was written Pre-COVID). An online experience? Do you want to work on-campus or off-campus? Accessible from home? Long drive? Short drive? Flight? Study abroad options?

A ton of these questions are easy to answer. Answer them once and then forget about them. Focus on the ones that matter.

Throughout this book, you're going to "meet" former students, young professionals, professors, and seasoned executives who have all been successful at carving out their own paths. And you'll hear some ridiculous stories from yours truly who fails enough, daily, to save you from any embarrassment you might feel in not knowing what your track is.

First of all…can we discuss something for a second? How old are you? 14? 15? 18? 23 even? WHO EVEN CARES? I'm 35 years old and still don't know what tomorrow looks like!

Have you ever heard of the phrase "paralysis by analysis?" Sure you have. If not, then you're welcome. Start using it. It's the theory that we tend not to make any moves in fear that we will make the wrong decision. So we do nothing so that we can't do the wrong thing. It's a phrase I've heard growing up, so it's not new. But, it is something that still plagues me. I have even not processed paperwork for a sale because I was afraid to.

Dude…seriously? (P.S. - I really hope the word "dude" is okay as a pronoun…I consider it gender-neutral as "I'm a dude…He's a dude… She's a dude…We're all dudes.") The lyrics, it's a fun song.

So, you may have heard of paralysis by analysis. Now, have you heard of "Getting your shoes dirty?" You absolutely have not... because I made it up a few years ago...and I ain't that famous.

"Getting your shoes dirty" means that you have to walk down a path...ANY path. Let me paint the picture for you, okay? This is where it gets fun.

You're moseying on the road of life, and all of a sudden, there's a fork in it. BOOM!

Now this road...can you picture it? It's a dirt road...super barren... with fields and trees all over. You can't see very far in either direction when you get to the fork. And the signs are vague. One points to the road that you should logically select, given the facts. And the other points to the road going in the complete other direction...maybe it's one that seems an alternative or something heartfelt and passionate. Maybe it LOOKS almost identical! Even worse!

You have to pick one path. And they are going to wind and weave and separate, drastically, and you might even be able to see the other road at certain points, etc. If you pick the wrong road, you can't cut through the fields and forests to get to the same point of the other road. You HAVE to stay on your road. You'll be in a completely different city. You'll get lost if you try to cut through the trees at any point.

So, what's your fear?

Your fear is that you're going to select a road, and it'll be the wrong one, right? Maybe your buddy or a group of buddies is going to be at the same intersection with you, watching you pick. After all, with social media nowadays, every decision we make is publicized and scrutinized, isn't it? Ugh...I hate social media...but that's another story for another book. I know we all have fun on it.

So, you make your choice. And you start walking.

Years later, you realize you've made the wrong choice. The dirt path you've taken was not what you thought it would be. You took a risk and you failed. You ABSOLUTELY cannot cut through the uncharted territory to get to the same point on another road. (Yes, we like uncharted territory, normally, but not in this case) Furthermore, upon choosing that path, there were other forks and intersections you'd made decisions about. Everything has molded you and taught you. So, you have to find your way back to that decision, step by step. And you do.

And when you get to the original intersection, you see your mates. You're afraid they are judging you, laughing at the decision you'd made. Posting, liking, commenting, etc. While they saved their energy by not making the "wrong" decision, you went ahead and spent your time and energy on yours. But do you want to know something? They didn't make the right decision either. If they did, they'd be down that other road. Or maybe they went down that other road and made some mistakes, too! That's why they are there!

I've had friends who have changed careers SEVERAL times, changed universities twice, been married and divorced and remarried, had children with a partner to separate and start a family with someone else.

Bottom Line: WHO CARES? Stop worrying about what people think! Ready for another metaphor?

I call this part of the equation the "Wedding Gown Complex." We're all getting ready for a wedding, and we're excited about how we look. And on the way there, we see that a hair fell out of place, or we got a stain on our tie, or our two socks are mismatched.

Ask yourself something. Do you really think anyone is looking at you? They are looking at the bride! And if not the bride, they are as focused on themselves as you are on YOURSELF. So stop worrying about what others think.

What should you be worrying about? Your shoes are FILTHY. Yup, that's right. They are covered in mud and dirt from your journey. You would think this is a bad thing, yes? It's not.

While your mates were paralyzed in that one spot, you were gaining experience. And while you can't take any shortcuts to get to the same spot on a new road, you have some great positives working in your favor: Your shoes are worn in.

- You know how to walk/run.
- Your experiences have helped you navigate one road; they'll help you navigate the next.

- You have lots of stories, wisdom, and all of that other great stuff to share!

We call these transferable skills. Stop worrying about the path. The path is going to be FUN. What you should be concerned about and focused on is the "end game." I had a great mentor who used Franklin Covey's 2nd Habit from *The 7 Habits of Highly Effective People,* which is to "Begin with the end in mind." (Pick up some of their books, too.) So what does that mean? Especially given the fact that every generation that we add to our workforce changes so rapidly…What does the end really look like?

Well, you can't pick a job as your "end." Your job won't exist in 15 years. Can you pick a life partner? Meh….let's stay away from the rising divorce rate. Family? Yikes…that may not look the way you intended it, either.

Let's…Start With Y.O.U!

Just you.

Do this for me, please:

1 - Let the room get quiet.
2 - Look in the mirror.
3 - Decide what you think is most important to you at this moment.
4 - Think about if that will be important to you during your last days.
5 - If it isn't, what will be?

Things to eliminate:

1 - Jobs
2 - Living locations
3 - Material possessions
4 - Particulars

Look…we're talking about the soul here. The core of your being! The reality is that you can't predict the people around you, the job you'll have, what you'll own, or where you'll be. None of these things are even important!

What you can predict is YOU. What will YOU be like? Will you be a person of integrity? Faith? Spirituality? Good health? Ruthless competitiveness? Strategic intuition? Kindness and heart? Family values? Wealth and connections? Intellect? Well, there is one way to find out—write your own obituary.

Worksheet: Obituary

You've lived a long life. You die peacefully in whatever state you would like, surrounded by whomever you'd like. What's it look like? Write your story.

_____
_____
_____
_____
_____
_____
_____
_____
_____
_____
_____
_____
_____
_____
_____
_____
_____
_____
_____
_____

Reflection

1. Are you proud of your story?

_____
_____
_____

2. What are you currently doing that's not part of the story?

_____
_____
_____

_____

3. What do you need to do to make that story a reality?
_____
_____
_____

Throughout each chapter, we're going to do a few things:

- Show you some examples of successes and failures from people I've encountered in my life
- Give you a "Professor's Pro Tip"
- Show you some statistics
- Provide a worksheet you can use to make that chapter a reality.

I think you've gotten enough from me on successes and failures. And I am going to try to make these chapters short and digestible. I struggle with attention myself. So I get it. But I also want to give you your money's worth.

I will mention that I've met some pretty awesome and successful folks who never went to college. If it's not for you, it's not for you. One such friend and colleague is one of the most successful and wealthiest people I know and was working at a pizzeria for years while my friends and I were dropping tens of thousands of dollars on college/university bills. So, if you're reading this book and realizing that none of this is for you…THAT IS OKAY. You'll still find some great skills and lessons here. Plus…you already bought the book so you may as well finish it.

Professor's Pro Tip (These are my own personal tips that can be helpful for you.)

Mark this book up. When you're reading, read actively. I teach in a state where some teachers actually TEACH speed reading. Let me break something down for you…speed reading isn't reading. Photographic memory is rare. We don't ALL have superhuman abilities. You know what's cool? Reading actively. Take notes, re-read things you didn't catch. Keep the room quiet or play instrumental music so you have fewer distractions. Focus. It's dope.

From the Experts (These help you understand the lessons from the chapter in a more concrete way.)

1. In 2019, 35% of the U.S. population had completed four years of college or more with an average of 47.4% of adults having earned a degree. For people who are 25 to 34 years old, the numbers are higher than the national average. In that age group, 50% of the population has some sort of a postsecondary degree (independence.edu).

2. The average U.S. household income is $87,864, and the median is $61,937 (fool.com). The median income is a tad over $31,000 (per person). This is from Google, 2020.

3. Reading is said to help improve short-term memory, focus, and concentration and reduce stress (various websites). It's also positively correlated with income, negatively correlated with crime and incarceration, etc. (medium.com).

CHAPTER 1
THE MOST IMPORTANT DECISION OF YOUR LIFE

There's a movie…I am almost certain it's the movie *He Got Game*. I'm an old dude so it's an old movie from the 1990s… Yuck, right? Funny enough, someone brought to my attention that I talked about the 1960s the same way young folks talk about the 1990s….Bruh…"I am on Tik Tok. I have a man purse. I drink hard seltzers. I listen to Lil Nas X." I'm progressive as hell. Don't do that to me.

Anyway, it's about this young basketball player who is trying to pick the right college, which is going to set him up for years of NBA basketball stardom, etc., etc. His father is a convict who has been asked to convince him to select a certain school. Oh, and he's in jail for the murder of his wife. Pretty heavy stuff, yeah?

So every time this high school basketball phenomenon meets someone, they say,

"This will be the most important decision of your life."

In fact…Oh yes! It was in like a montage!

"This…THIS…this…*this*…" - various humans

"Will…Will be…Will be…" - those same humans

Then they get choppy.

"Be…"
"Be…"
"The most…"
"THE MOST"
"Important…"
"Decision…"
"…of your life."

"This will be the most important decision of your life."

Well…here's what's up. Do you remember when I said the stuff about the things you'll pick that won't be the right things and that's okay? You have no idea where you're going to be 30 years from now. So how are you supposed to pick the perfect first step? You're not. You're just going to do the best that you can.

It's…going…to be fine. You have no idea where your career is going to take you. But you need to make sure that YOU are intact at all times, that you're building skills, and that you are doing something to progress, always.

The reality is that your career is going to take you to a million places you never thought it could. When I was earning my MBA at a small private college on Long Island, Molloy College, there were lots of working executives, etc. in the program. Now, I am going to sound old for a second. Not many students earned an MBA directly after a BA or BS for several reasons:

• Schools weren't desperate for enrollment the way they are now.
• Students weren't being turned down for jobs the way they are with a Bachelor's Degree today.

In fact, the MBA has become such a commodity today that it's almost obsolete. I'd rather get a degree in quantitative analysis or big data today. But, alas, an MBA was all the rave back then. So once I started my first job after graduating in the world of banking (I actually had another job for less than two months after I graduated...but we won't even bring that one up at this point. It wasn't the career choice for me), I enrolled in the MBA program.

Our executive MBA program took two years to complete. So by the second year, I'd gone from a sales role to my position as the Assistant Director of Training and then left that bank to work in marketing and sales at Yahoo! Inc. Prior to that, I found it very easy to progress to other roles, as well, in and before college. Now, mind you, I was a young graduate and an even younger MBA. Most folks earning that degree were 10, 20, and 30 years my senior.

So one of our final projects in Organizational Behavior was to complete this career timeline to show folks where we'd progress. Everyone else had lines that looked more like stock charts. Ups and Downs. You know what I am talking about right? Let me show you one.

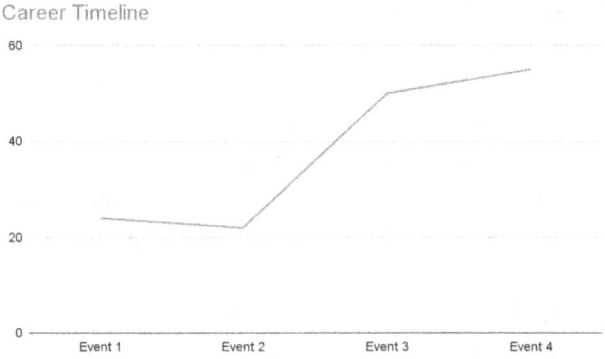

And, I remember thinking, "Why on earth would anyone choose to show a graph like that? We go up...always up! We just get better and better every year. Right?"

I get up in front of the classroom and give my presentation about career trajectory. Straight up! To the moon! See you there, Elon! A straight direct correlation between years and growth. Easy peasy. Now, give me my A so I can finish the next few classes and get started! Everyone clapped. It was exactly what I knew would happen.

But then something interesting happened. After class, a bunch of folks came up to me and said, "Oh my goodness, you're so brave. That was a great line to draw in your presentation. I wish I could think like you."

Ermmm….Did I miss something? Yeah, I did. I was 22 at the time, and it would take 10+ years to figure it out.

What was it?

NOBODY has a career like that. Not only had I taken demotions to go to larger companies, moved around laterally, started at the bottom when I arrived in different industries, and even lost my job, but some of the most successful people I have ever worked for had gone through all of those things, as well. I am talking millionaires! But you won't figure that out until you've lived it as I have. Or at least seen it.

So, how do you prepare for a career you don't even know you'll have yet? We develop "transferable skills." Building those skills is all that matters. Otherwise known as twists and turns.

Here's an example of some twists and turns. One of my colleagues, Dr. Matthew Miraglia, owns a very successful security organization and app, the first and only of its kind in one of the most controversial and exploding markets to exist…ever—public security for schools and venues. In the wake of the mass shootings we've experienced in the past few years, it's a market that is completely foreign to some folks. But he's changing the world and doing it in a way that builds his reputation and wealth. But Dr. Miraglia didn't decide to be an entrepreneur overnight…

When I met Matthew Miraglia, I could tell you a few very important things about him—he was intelligent, he was respectful, and he was disciplined. He made those impressions on me in the first few seconds I'd known him. And they were integral parts of his success, no matter what he did.

Miraglia began his career in the military. He was specifically a weapons of mass destruction specialist, and from what I understand of it, he was trained (and then trained others) on how to fight a war amidst nuclear fallout. If you had no resources, what would you do?

Where would you turn first? That's what Miraglia specialized in. When I learned that, I had to learn more about him!

After I'd initially met Dr. Miraglia, he invited my ex-wife and me to have dinner with him and his wife.

Wait a second! Ex-wife? You made a decision that didn't end up the way you'd planned? Yup! I sure did! Twists and Turns... Moving on.

Miraglia was teaching at a business school for a private college in Westchester County, one at which I had recently become Program Director. He'd invited us to dinner right away. He kept calling me "boss" and, technically, I suppose I was. But I never thought of myself as anyone's boss, and in academia...nobody really cares. Most folks are so pretentious and self-centered that they don't actually care who their boss is...which is one reason that our university system is a wreck at the moment. Everyone is just going their own way. Not to mention, I have always managed people 10-15 or even 30 years older than me. I always thought of us as a team. And I certainly learn from my team members every day...from banking to marketing to academia.

Miraglia is no different. I learned lots from him. He is precise, has had an illustrious career, and puts his heart and soul into everything he does. You can't tell him to do anything without him doing it to the best of his ability and being ultra-competitive...not because he wants to beat you. It's because he wants to serve his team and do the best job. (As an aside, google a guy by the name of Brandon Burlsworth. He had a great *Sports Illustrated* article written about him, as well as a movie made after his death. He was dedicated to everything he did before his untimely passing. I've included a link at the end of this chapter. THAT is Dr. Matthew Miraglia.) He had such a knack for entrepreneurship, business, and strategy. Naturally, he was great in the military since he left as a corporal. But there was so much more to him.

When he told me how he started his career, my first question was, "How on earth did you end up here?" Well, there are plenty of ways it could have happened. Let's figure it out:

After his impressive military career, and upon Miraglia's return to the States after his time in the military, he began a post in the Westchester Police Department in an anti-terrorism unit. His job was in counter-terrorism in the wake of 9-11. As he retired from the Academy, he earned two Master's Degrees and began to teach after his time served there. The Corporate and Homeland Security Department was kind of without a home at our college. Did it belong with the criminal justice folks? Often, those departments, due to cybersecurity components, tend to fall into business and management schools. And the folks who run them have to adjust their thinking. So that's where it ended up.

But that was not the case with Miraglia. Miraglia was a natural entrepreneur and very structured in his thinking, which is not at all what most entrepreneurs are. He'd already had a budding consulting company. He was very spirited in business. I knew this because when my Dean asked me who I wanted to share an office with, there was no question—it was Dr. Matthew Miraglia. Want to hear another mistake? I had a larger office than the Dean! But then I bragged about it until some of the other faculty members complained, and that's when I was forced to share it. Hey...go figure. Life happens. But I was glad to share one with Miraglia.

One example of how Miraglia combined creativity and discipline that I noted was how he completely overtook our social entrepreneurship competition:

We had five different teams of ten students who were all competing for funding from our department to go to a national competition. The task at hand was to create a business that had some sort of social component...it could be a green initiative, showcase other cultures, etc. I created a mobile thrift store with my students, and we were marginally successful. We did events and sold our goods every other Friday in various spots on campus. Everything we took in was donated by students and faculty, and we sold it all for really low prices. My team of awesome passionate entrepreneurs would have won the whole darn competition if not for Miraglia's team. Want to hear the best part? I remember that I specifically could have sworn, out of all five teams, that his team would end up in last place by the way his students talked about the business. Specifically, about him!

"He's a tyrant! He's working us too hard!"
"We don't even know if he knows what he's doing!"

I thought, for sure, that he was going to be at the bottom of the five teams. That is until I saw what he'd done...

Miraglia helped his team create an event company that focused solely on showcasing other cultures. That included nationalities, genders, and even professions (using his connections in law enforcement, the military, etc.) Why was this so important? Because we happened to be working at a school with almost zero student life. So to charge a small fee for a meal and some activities was actually BRILLIANT. Miraglia saw a need and filled it using resources he already had, a skill undoubtedly picked up whilst solving problems in the military. And to showcase other cultures was a very smart idea, as well, considering our school was a minority-driven school. Inclusion was embraced.

Did Miraglia pick up some ideas from the folks around him in the business school? Possibly. But what he did next was, without a doubt, his assertion of will, based on his own knowledge, skills, and abilities. And he learned many of these skills in the military, which...yes...was his first decision made after high school.

Miraglia loved working with students and felt the drive they had for entrepreneurship and creativity. He believed in our students so much that he hired a few after graduation to partner with him on his app. Using his fees as a consultant and his pension, which were all additional income, he was able to fund this app project and turn it into a multi-million dollar business.

So why am I telling you this story? Because Dr. Miraglia felt it important to build his discipline, knowledge, and skills up after high school. He did not feel it important to finish his life in the military. But that one decision set the stage for a lifetime and career in education, training, and an entrepreneurial venture that would make him financially successful for life. Was it the most important decision of his life to join the military? No. It was the first of many he'd make that set him on his path, and the many decisions he made after that used his transferable skills. Let's break them down:

- Discipline: Let me tell you. When I have three incomes, I spend four. That's why I have seven. Miraglia lived on the income he needed to while investing the rest in his app.
- Chain of Command: Miraglia knew well enough that our Dean brought in a team of folks to help administration. He was the first person to invite me to dinner, and we struck up a friendship immediately. I gave him no preferential treatment, but he was easy to work with. I found myself bouncing ideas off of him and spending time after work picking his brain on what was best for our faculty.
- Knowledge of Criminal Justice and Military Systems: Do you see how everything Miraglia did revolved around this?

  ◦ Teaching at the Corporate Security program?
  ◦ His Consulting firm and app?
  ◦ His project with his students making use of police and firefighters he knew?
  ◦ He's also an expert on various news stations.

With each new role he took on, he used his old skills and added new ones. This is something you need to think about now. Most hard skills you need right now won't be needed a few years from now but the ability to read a room, be a self-starter, have discipline, etc. will!

And you'll make those decisions constantly. We often find ourselves making decisions that will impact our lives greatly. The funny part is that we don't often comprehend the impact of those decisions until years later. Without hindsight and wisdom, how could we, right? But you'll note that some of the decisions in your life will make you exactly who you are at 25, 30, 40, and beyond.

That was definitely the case with my mentor and friend, Dr. Robert Valli. Valli loves to tell the story of how he decided to go to the University of California, Berkeley. Now, if you are from the West Coast, you'll likely know it's arguably one of the best schools in California. (Let's start the debate…who says Stanford?) Let's compromise…it's the #1 public institution. If you're from elsewhere, you may have heard it mentioned amongst some of the Ivy's. Long story short: its rank is the #22 school in the country.

Valli got into Berkeley…read that again…Dr. Robert Valli got into Berkeley at the age of 17. And it wasn't his first choice. Nope, his first choice was a school in Colorado that offered him a baseball scholarship. At the time, Valli loved baseball more than anything, and he wanted to go to a school that would allow him to play ball. This smaller (not as prestigious) school in Colorado offered Rob a baseball scholarship. Rob took it and was ready to head out of Northern California.

Just as he was ready to swing away, Valli received word that he would not be playing ball. The baseball team at his new home in Colorado had been cut, leaving him without a scholarship. Sure, he could attend but it wasn't the school that excited him, it was his ability to play ball there.

So Rob had to think fast. He decided to pack up his buddy's car, a buddy who was going to be getting an apartment and attending a community college a few hours away. At that moment, his friend spoke up…

"Don't be a fool," he said. "So many people want to be in your position. You got into one of the best schools in the country. That's where you need to be."

And so it was. Rob Valli went to Berkeley. He had an incredible career in consumer products and then banking. He earned his MBA from Stanford University (now can we say he went to the best school in California and one of the best in the country?) and his Ph.D. from Cambridge (arguably one of the best universities in the world).

Valli has pioneered in academia, investment banking, research, and entrepreneurship. He has absolutely had peaks and valleys…get it… valleys? I know you're laughing. He completely halted his career when he quit his job to become a Ph.D. He has had failed startups. He has also been wildly successful in every single thing he's done. All of the skills he has such as:

- Emotional Intelligence
- Culture
- Analytical Skills
- Free thinking
- Finances
- Delegation
- Sales

came from the combination of these programs and his career that spanned from banking to startups to research. Valli is thoughtful and passionate. He is kind and generous. He is also absolutely brilliant. Sure, he learned some of these things at the three most prestigious schools in the world. But it was these things that also led him there. And his decision to start his career at Berkeley propelled him. It didn't make or break him. But it got him to where he wanted to be much faster. And that time is priceless.

FROM THE EXPERTS

1. The Cappex College Admissions Counseling Survey says that the average recommended number of applications from high school counselors is 5.9. They say that 90% of students submit less than 10 applications.

2. The majority of schools admit most of the people who apply to them (pewresearch.org)

3. In 2016, the most recent year for which statistics are available, the Bureau of Labor Statistics reported that 69.7 percent of students who graduated high school in 2016 were enrolled in college.

PROFESSOR'S PRO TIP

I volunteered for admissions when I did my undergrad. As a senior, I got to interview prospective students as they were applying and making their decisions. I recall there was a statistic we would rattle off.

I forget the number, but it was something like "60% of students who come for an official visit wind up choosing our college." Now I don't know if it's because they were so spellbound by our amazing institution (that's not sarcasm, I literally fell in love during my tour) or if those who were serious about us popped in for a visit. So it would make sense that they enrolled.

My suggestion to you is that you MUST take some time to visit a few schools, especially the ones you're serious about. Visit them all if you can. If you don't, cross them off the list. They won't get a fair shake. In fact, try to visit before you apply. Yes, we live in a virtual world now and especially with COVID just winding down, everyone still wants to do things on-screen.

Don't.

Eventually, we will be back to a certain normalcy. And each generation tends to lose the ability to interact in person. That is the first skill you should be building.

I get it; it's tough. I visited a college fair once in the inner city, and the counselor made an announcement. "This is like visiting 15 colleges at once. None of y'all will have an experience like this again." That made me sad. I spoke to several students who wouldn't visit any schools before applying or attending, and most of them stayed close to home. So if you do get the opportunity to visit colleges, cherish that opportunity. And do more than talk to people. Stay overnight if you can. Visit a class. You'll thank yourself later.

Complete the chart on the following page after you've visited several colleges. Compare and contrast them to better determine your own interests and priorities.

12 THE COLLEGE ADMISSION

College/University	1	2	3	4	5
Location					
Commuter or Resident					
Public or Private					
Size					
Majors/Minors					
Social Life Rating					
Mock Class Rating					
Tuition					
Scholarship					

*https://vault.si.com/vault/1999/06/28/almost-perfect-arkansas-lineman-brandon-burlsworth-dedicated-himself-to-doing-everything-flawlessly-when-something-finally-went-wrong-it-cost-him-a-bright-nfl-futureand-his-life

CHAPTER 2
YOU CAN'T HAVE YOUR CAKE AND EAT IT, TOO

Cake...isn't that what they call money? Oh, no...that's bread! Okay, well...what I'm trying to say is that you can't spend all of your money and keep it. So you need to really be careful about where it goes and what it goes into. And it starts with when you make your college decision.

I know I'm going to sound like a dad right now...and I'm not yet, but the value of the dollar is important to learn. Check it out: we all have this notion in our brain that we haven't made real money yet and after college, things will be different. WRONG. After college, you could be in crippling debt or you can be in a better financial situation than most and start your career off with a lower balance than the rest of your cohorts.

By the way, I did not understand this when I entered or exited college. My father allowed me access to my savings account when I entered college, and I spent thousands of dollars before my freshman year was over. Most of my savings were gone. *But it's all good,* I thought. *I'll make so much money when I graduate, this won't matter.* This same thinking led me through to my senior year where I spent almost every dollar I had. I had to ask my father for a loan, upon graduation, so that I could pay a credit card bill.

Don't think the way I thought. Think about your college choice the same way you'd think about buying lunch. Sure, you want the best lunch in town. Maybe a little steak? Lobster? Sushi? But is that really in your budget, every day? Sometimes that two-for-two deal at Burger King looks just as dope because you can keep that extra money for the weekend. For a year, I did that. I took my lunch money and got the least expensive things on the dollar menu. And at the end of each week, I had a few extra bucks…which of course I spent…like an idiot.

But, you…you have this book…full of all of my screw-ups. So you can do it all the RIGHT way, right? Right! And, think with your…

- Brain
- Heart
- And Gut

NOT JUST ONE OF THEM!

That was the case with Billy Johanson. Billy was one of my students, very briefly, at a private college in Westchester, New York. I have to make that distinction because Billy was probably one of the few students I could barely help. But not because he wouldn't learn from me. We had a few conversations inside and outside of class. To be honest, he was far too wise for me to help much more than I already had.

When I met Billy, he was transferring to a college I was working at from a very similar school on Long Island. Both institutions were unique in that they were on the hunt for the absolute best students they could find and had really aggressive academic scholarship models to bring them in. The reason he was transferring was that most of his mentorship team had left his former college. But let's examine how that happened and how he used his brain, heart, and gut to make that decision.

I'm not one to pry into my students' personal lives, but I can certainly make some inferences based on what I see. Johanson had an upbringing of wealth. His father worked in finance, he lived in a wealthy part of Long Island, he dressed in perfectly pressed high-end clothing, etc., etc. He also had mannerisms one would pick up from others with money.

Johanson also grew up in a very pure and genuine home, with very caring parents who taught him how to make sound decisions. In the few times I met them, it was clear that they trusted him implicitly because they'd given him very many tools to do the best possible job as his own compass.

You need to know these things because Johanson's first choice was to go to a very strong Business program in Boston...a very expensive business program, as well. When he was approached by a small Long Island institution to join their Business School on a major scholarship, his heart would tell him that it wasn't where he wanted to be. But he discussed his finances with his family, and the scholarship was just too powerful to pass up.

Johanson was going to miss out on a traditional college experience, but he would graduate from his four-year institution with nearly zero debt. And because of that, I'm pretty sure his family agreed to get him a much nicer car so that he could commute to school. Either that or the kid was a baller because he was driving a BMW. Johanson definitely used his brain. He also had to think to himself the inevitable 3.8 - 4.0 GPA he'd earn in a program that was a bit less rigorous and more personalized would set him up for a great job and potential graduate school scholarships.

At the time, I was adjunct teaching at the school where he was learning. Unfortunately, try as I may, I was unable to gain full-time employment there, which was my goal: leave the corporate world and teach our youth. Despite our Dean's best efforts, the committee that made full-time hires wasn't interested. Two years later, there would be a change for both Billy and myself.

Fortunately for me, our Dean was poached to head to another institution where he'd have the ability to make hiring decisions, and we had a really awesome committee of faculty who were more open-minded when it came to young, spunky, non-researched faculty. I was hired and a few members of Billy's mentorship team came along with me. Now, at this point, I was a non-entity for Billy, but there were some other faculty members who had helped mold him over the course of his first few years, helping him find internships and select his major. He wanted to work on Wall Street but decided to be an accounting major and earn his CPA, working for a Big Four accounting firm, particularly publicly auditing banks so that he could then move into investment banking. Smart…again, the whole brain thing, right?

Well, Billy's dreams started to change around him as a few of his mentors left his institution to join the new regime at another school. There were no hard feelings there, but an entrepreneurial faculty will want to join a new "startup" department if there's room to have fun. Billy had to use his gut and decided to take a few tours of the competing school. He began weighing his options and thinking about what his career might look like if he stayed at his previous institution or if he joined this new one.

Johanson was on the fence. All things considered, his finances would probably be similar at either school. He had considerable scholarships at both, given his great academics and intangibles but he had to start thinking about what his next 40 years would look like, not just the current four. And a few of the folks who'd helped mold him were moving on.

It wasn't until one of his favorite faculty members, and arguably the most connected in the fields of consulting and investment banking, switched programs that Johanson decided to move, as well. He used his heart to make an informed decision about what his best options were, weighed the pros and the cons, and ultimately planted the seeds that would grow him into one of the most successful graduates I've ever seen.

Johanson had escalating internships at firms like UBS and even Goldman Sachs. That last one…be careful and reread it. That's the top internship an aspiring investment banker, accountant, or consultant can possibly have. The only place that would trump it would be Google. Johanson got there through incredible networking and being the absolute best candidate in our small program, a program he knew he would dominate in and where he could save money. He was the only non-Ivy League student there. And I hear he outperformed his comrades there, as well.

Johanson then completed 150 credit hours of undergraduate classes and earned his CPA without a Master's Degree, which is something that is rare and very interesting. I remember him telling me why he was doing it...yes, as I was supposed to be advising him. Hah! Shouldn't I have been telling HIM what to do?

Basically, the way it works is that, in New York State, you need 150 credit hours to sit for your CPA. Most people assume that means you need a Master's Degree, either in Accounting or Business. Johanson didn't want to pay for his entire Master's Degree, and he also wanted one from a top 20 school. He knew he wouldn't be scholarshipped as well as he wanted to be directly after college but assumed that whichever firm hired him would have a reimbursement program. This is pretty normal. The largest banks and accounting firms will cover some or all of your MBA or Master's Degree if you achieve a certain grade each semester and you stay with that firm for X amount of years. He didn't want to stay an accountant, so an MBA was his best option. He crammed 150 credit hours into four years (with a little help from his AP and college courses in high school) and decided he'd wait on his Master's Degree. And he absolutely took advantage of his academic scholarship by jamming as much as he could into it.

Upon graduation, Johanson had close to a half dozen Fortune 50 level offers, ranging from Big Four accounting firms to banks to consulting agencies. He ultimately decided to go with one of the Big Four, but to their consulting branch, forgoing becoming a public accountant as a way into investment banking. Consulting and investment banking are, without a doubt, two of the most lucrative career options that anyone can take.

Billy and I check in once in a while. I'm happy now to call him a colleague, as I was but a few years older than him when I worked with him. From what I have heard through the career grapevine and him, he moved up a few rungs at this very large consulting firm by bringing in small to midsize clients (something NOBODY at his level does). He parlayed that success to become a much more integral part of a smaller consulting firm. He lives on the East Coast with his girlfriend, and he definitely manages his life the same way he managed his money while making his college decision: with mentor and family counsel, conservatively, and working his butt off to make sure he's at the top of his class.

Do you see how, if you create intelligent money habits, you'll carry them on through college and beyond? Okay, okay, I know I'm sounding preachy but this is something even I have trouble with. I get a signing bonus of $20,000…I spend $25,000. I get a raise, I buy a car. Don't do that. Don't be like me. Thank goodness I've been happy and content in the amount of money I've made. But now that I'm transitioning to entrepreneurship, I wish I had all of the money I'd spent on cruises and cars in my bank account!

Nobody exemplifies thrifty spending and saving like some of the Wall Street folks I know. They made millions upon millions of dollars, but it required absolute discipline in their earlier years. Imagine getting multiple paychecks for $10,000, $20,000, and $50,000 weekly in your 20s? Yeah, I got a few of those. I spent them on comic books and collectibles or some sort of ridiculous silliness. But these guys? Absolute discipline.

I had a mentor in my time at one of my private universities who was just an absolute wealth of knowledge. I mean, I could tell you so many stories of just sitting in his office and randomly stealing tidbits of awesome. He was once cornered during a job interview by some jerk who said he "wasted his Ivy League education" with a degree in Mandarin Chinese. This was the 80s, by the way. His response when asked, "Why did you get that stupid degree?"

"Well," he quipped. "So that I can speak to a billion more people than you can."

So…like…yeah…WOWZA! Oh, by the way, he got the damn job.

I learned a lot from my mentor of three years. He even taught me how to create my own Personal Advisory Board (see Chapter 3). But one of my favorite pieces of advice he didn't realize he'd bestowed upon me was how to be a little stingy when you need to be.

My mentor had a co-worker at that same job with the jerk who asked about his degree in Mandarin. This guy was a little older, a bit non-traditional (most folks who join investment banks like this one were early-to-mid 20s, fresh off an MBA. He had apparently spent a few years after getting his degree(s) just living life. He rode the rails, traveled the country, and just grew wiser (yes, for those still reading, wisdom and intelligence are different!).

My mentor, as a young person, had just started his job and was struggling to make ends meet financially. His wise, older buddy said something to the effect of, "Hey, man, are you coming to the retirement plan meeting tomorrow at work?" He replied that he couldn't. He didn't make enough money to actually save and put into his retirement plan. What? An investment banker who couldn't invest? Yeah, it happens all the time. Especially when you're starting out. At any job, it's really challenging to make enough money to save. Well, my mentor's new mentor wasn't about to let that happen.

"Meet me at the grocery store after work," he said. "We'll figure it out."

What he did was simple…almost too simple. And, you're probably not going to like it. I didn't like it when I first read *The Millionaire Next Door*. Ever read that book? It basically talks about how millionaires live simply. They buy less expensive shoes, suits, watches, etc. They don't take very expensive vacations. Everything they do is tapered.

Yuck! Why? What's the point of making money if you can't spend it, right?

Yeah…the point of making money is to make your life easier so that the older you get the less you need to think about money. We think it's so that we can live lavishly. Most who live lavishly actually don't have money!

Yeah, yeah…I get it. Lame, right?

Well, what my mentor learned at the grocery store was a little bit more than not spending money on suits. His friend/mentor dragged him through the bulk food aisle and showed him a few things:

- Bulk Rice
- Canned Salmon
- Dry beans and legumes

He said, "Live on this until you don't have to." And that was it. In that one move, he taught my mentor that you can save money into your retirement plan.

It's a simple concept, but that doesn't make it easy to execute.

Being smart with your money is just as important as making it, if not more so. Making intelligent (and wise) decisions. This is a fact to remember for both the college process and post-college. I can't tell you how many folks in my life make and have made way less money than me and live way better. It's because when I make $100,000 I spend $102,000! Don't do that.

If this pandemic has taught us anything, it's that you have to be intelligent about how you spend your money. That includes career training. Look at folks who go to trade school…making way more money than folks who go to prestigious liberal arts schools! Now I am not saying you need to change your life and be an electrician if you want to go to a traditional four-year residential college. What I am saying is that there are plenty of those and, if your school isn't in the top 50 in the country (maybe top 25), nobody is going to care what the school ranking is. So take the opportunity to measure costs and benefits. What are their opportunities for career services and job placement? Scholarships and grants? Work-study or on-campus jobs? What do graduates say about the debt they incur? Sometimes it can be worth it. Is it?

FROM THE EXPERTS

1. The cost of college has increased by more than 25% in the last 10 years. - CNBC.com

2. In 2018, college graduates earned weekly wages that were 80% higher than those of high school graduates. - The Bureau of Labor Statistics, 2018

3. The average in-state student attending a public four-year institution spends $25,615 for one academic year. The average cost of in-state tuition alone is $9,580; out-of-state tuition averages $27,437. The average traditional private university student spends a total of $53,949 per academic year, $37,200 of it on tuition and fees. Taking into account student loan interest and

loss of income, the ultimate cost of a Bachelor's Degree may exceed $400,000. - EducationData.org

PROFESSOR'S PRO TIP

"That was the best four years of my life." So many folks discuss college/university as if it was a four-year vacation. Hey, did I have fun in college? Sure I did. Did I have a little too much fun? Sure…maybe, but it wasn't the best four years of my life. There were moments of "best" level stuff. But my college, Siena College, is without a doubt a great institution that set me up for years of success. They know they have a hefty price tag. But their newer of several taglines alludes to "4 years for 40 years of success." In other words, pay the four years of bills because you know you'll have tons of success in your lifetime.

Do your research. Yes, go with your gut, but also understand that universities are great sales folks. Speak to as many alumni as possible, current students, etc. Don't just take someone's word for it. I remember a student told me about some midwest school that was recruiting him because he wanted to study abroad and they had "The best study abroad program in the country." I'd never heard of this place…and they didn't.

Gut. Heart. Brain. Use all three.

The charts on the following pages allow you an opportunity to narrow your choices further and gather additional information to help you to make your final decision.

Worksheet

Once you've narrowed your school down to the 2-3 you're really serious about, I want you to start collecting data on:

- Grants and scholarships they're offering
- Price of tuition
- Price of room and board
- Other costs
- Entry-level salaries after college
- Placement rate after college

And use the following to find that data:

- U.S. News
- Other college data sites
- Alumni
- Current Students
- Web Review
- Data published by the university or college

YOU CAN'T HAVE YOUR CAKE AND EAT IT, TOO

School Name	1	2	3	4	5
Tuition					
Scholarship/Grants Offered					
Room and Board Costs					
Other Costs					
Placement Rates and Avg Salary Post Graduation					

CHAPTER 3
MENTORSHIP, NETWORKING, AND SOCIAL NETWORKING

So now you have your college or university, and it's affordable. Let's start making use of it. It's never too early to start networking. I don't care where you are. It should be natural, and it should come easily, eventually. A mentor of mine said, "Networking is not about asking for favors from people you've just met. It's building genuine connections and being of service. Years later, when you do ask for a connection or favor, it should be as natural as asking a friend."

Contacts to keep in and after college should definitely be an art form and a science. Knowing who to stay in touch with, how often to contact, when to reach out, and how to do so is often challenging. I have a colleague I have lunch with 1-2 times a year. I call him a mentor, and he calls me a friend. I still don't see him as an equal, and he insists that I stop putting him on a pedestal. At some point, he'll probably get annoyed with my praise. Even I need to learn how to balance relationships! I can honestly say that I have only received one or two jobs from applying blind. The rest have been through my network of contacts.

Learning how to really connect with folks is super important. That balance has to be perfect so that we can remain friends with folks without seeming desperate, but sometimes we are, and that's okay!

We've also got into this quantitative game of social media…followers, likes on Instagram…and then we connect on Tik Tok or Facebook (yawn, I know I sound old). But try asking one of your new friends to buy a tee-shirt for your fundraiser or to help you find a job. I promise you that not many will because you're a number to them.

Let me tell you about one of my most charismatic and charming students. The art of building relationships is not lost on him. He's also one hell of a presenter, probably built from that same empathy. The kid didn't have a date for his senior prom (either by choice or not, we don't care). Instead of just showing up to the prom hall as his senior class president, he had his friends and family dress up as secret service people in suits with headsets. He filmed himself with a motorcade of black SUVs from his home to his prom. Now, THAT is style. But, I digress!

I can't have favorite students, but Donavion Thomas is a unique dude I'm fond of. Donavion began his time at our small private university in 2014 in a very similar position to most of our students: no wealth to speak of, mediocre grades, and very little knowledge of how the college process works. Furthermore, he had no idea how college was going to place him in the job market but followed his peers, blindly, into the education pool. I say this with some skepticism because I feel most college and university salespeople will display their confidence that their brand will help you land a job, but very few have actually been part of that process or understand how challenging it really is. This is a reality you need to be aware of. Admissions representatives are confident in their Career Services Department because they have to be.

We, however, were Deans and faculty members with connections. And we did actually have the connections we said we did. We told Donavion that he would have mentorship and the opportunity to make a name for himself. We also guaranteed him nothing but effort on our end. I feel that will instill more confidence in a student than to tell him "Don't worry, I'll get you a job." There's no way we know whether or not that will actually come to fruition. It's like guaranteeing a date with your best friend. You can guarantee that you'll bother them about it until they make a decision. But anyone who says "It's definitely happening" has no idea of the probability and is trying to close the conversation and close you as a person. I just happened to be the junior person on an amazing team of faculty members with probably 200+ years of experience and high-level connections that go along with those years. So we had a decent formula in place to help our hungry students, and Donavion was hungry, which was the only factor that separated him from most of his peers and it landed him a spot in our elite honors program, a program his grades alone wouldn't have gotten him into.

I struggled with Donavion that first year. Not because he was difficult, because he wasn't. I could tell he grew up with strong parents. Though they did not live together, I could see that they each taught him firm lessons about life, work, and personal relationships; and anyone who tells you those three things aren't related will likely be failing at least one of them. No, I struggled with Donavion because he had a clear vision about what he wanted his college years to look like, but he hadn't factored in his disadvantage. He had a lower incoming GPA than our other honors students and was at a non-ranked school with little brand recognition. And there are too many statistics not to talk about the fact that he was a student of diversity from a New York City borough. There's no way he could act like a rich white kid from Westchester or Nassau County who went to Villanova or Ithaca and expect to land a job from their Alumni network or a neighbor. (I say these things not to be funny. They are experiences I, myself, lived through as I came from an upper-middle-class suburb and relied on my class ring to land me an internship in college.)

No, Donavion struggled because he wanted to do it all—join a fraternity, run our student government, have fun, have a girlfriend, etc., etc. I'm an approachable administrator. It's what makes me "me." I hope that as I hit my 40s, I can still have the same level of "cool factor" as I did in my 20s. But my car is a lot slower, and my hair is a lot thinner. I also can't understand why we say things like "fleek" so I tend to rely on my "old man" attitude to get the laughs in the classroom that I used to get by talking about a fun weekend activity. But I do still tend to be a mentor for my students in all areas where I can appropriately help and Donavion has spent many hours in my office talking about classes, extra-curricular activities, and even dating. I remember, specifically, an instance in which we discussed another mentored student of mine and if he should ask her on a date. We went through the pros and cons of romance with someone you take classes with, free time, career distractions, etc. These are questions a father might answer. I was so pleased and honored to be able to give Donavion my opinion on so many subject areas, in and out of the classroom. It requires a certain level of trust between student and faculty and is not easy to replicate or scale.

This trust is important to note because, during the very first year of his freshman experience, I asked Donavion to take a leap of faith and trust me in a very specific circumstance regarding his career. Our college had multiple campuses, ranging in location, size, and atmosphere (urban versus suburban, demographics of students, etc.). It was important that our top students visited our two main campuses in the suburbs and in the heart of New York City. Donavion had come to class that day with his colleagues. It was a marketing class. He was dressed appropriately for class: jeans, plaid shirt, crisp clean pair of work boots. Donavion had a very cool humility about him in everything he did. But if you got to know him, he knew exactly what he was doing. I remember we had a conversation about him choosing a dish at dinner, and he said that there was no reason to rush a decision. Everything he ate had to be delicious otherwise, why eat it? Very smart guy. I mean…he did this at every meal we ate together…eye roll. Anyway, back to the trust situation.

Afternoon marketing class had just started, and I received an email from my Dean. (To be honest, I had received it late the night before but was prepping for class and taught that morning. I hadn't checked my emails thoroughly.) Students were working on an independent project, and I looked down at my work phone to see that there was an event going on at our Manhattan campus that evening. A few senior-level management consultants were coming to campus to meet with our MBA students. Again, I need to reiterate: small unbranded school, this is not an everyday thing.

"Chris, please see if some of our top undergraduates can meet with them, as well. Let's fill the room with talent since they've come all this way."

Again, not something that happens often, even at well-branded schools.

So, I looked around the room. The first person I'd thought of was Donavion. His goal was to work in management consulting or investment banking. This was a long shot for any student, but I wanted to make sure I entertained his dreams and helped him as much as I could. He had the drive and charisma, but not the brand in education.

While in class, I took one look at his attire. It wouldn't work. He was wearing jeans, Timberland boots, and a plaid shirt. Perfectly fine to wear for class, but he couldn't meet them like that. Our suburban campus, where his dorm room was, was over an hour away, each way. If he'd left class at that moment, he'd just barely make it back in time to catch the event, and he'd miss the rest of class if he did. No, it just wouldn't work.

I ruled him out because to ask him to go home or buy clothes would be too much to ask of anyone. Donavion's father was on strike, and I knew he didn't have a ton of money to throw around on a train ticket or new clothes. I took another look around the room. Most of my students weren't dressed properly to meet the consultants that evening. But there were two young women who just so happened to be wearing professional clothing. A button-up and a dress. They would present well, at least. They were in my honors class and I knew them well. They were intelligent and driven. But were they interested? A brief conversation with them revealed that:

1. They were, in fact, not interested in meeting the consultants.
2. They had evening plans, which is why they were dressed well.

Well, shoot…I needed to give the opportunity to someone. And Donavion really did have the drive and want. Maybe I could ask him. Maybe we could figure something out.

"Donavion…chat for a second?"

"Sure thing, Professor…"

"Hey, look, I know you want to meet some consultants. Some senior-level management consultants will be on campus soon. Had I known earlier, I could have told you to wear a suit to class today. I screwed up and didn't check my email early enough. Otherwise, I'd have texted you before you left campus. The reason I didn't come to you originally is that you want your first impression to be in professional attire. Is there any way you can find something to wear before this thing happens? Borrow something?"

"Uh…" he said. "Give me five minutes."

Donavion went out to the hallway and called his father. His father was on strike with a major telecom company and I didn't ask about their financial situation, but I had my doubts that it was excellent. Still, when he came back into the classroom, he told me his father put his credit card down at a nearby clothing store. He was instructed to get a pair of pants and a pair of shoes, tuck in his passable plaid shirt, and be ready to interview. He asked if he could take time from class, and I said "Absolutely, no problem."

Donavion came back to the classroom looking business casual: slacks, shoes, shirt tucked in. Sharp!

It was a great transformation, but I still had my doubts that he'd be taken seriously. He was an undergraduate student from a small private college and he wasn't cum laude or 4.0. What he had was unique—charisma and some serious confidence. He needed to sparkle and he didn't. Still, it was a great effort.

When the graduate students who would be meeting with the consultants came into the building that afternoon, I was just wrapping up class. They were dressed in suits. I knew they would be. I cringed.

"Donavion, here…" I said. "Take my sport coat and tie. It'll match what you've got on…sort of."

Donavion went into the interview/meeting and I am sorry to say, I didn't even stick around to be there after some light prep-work with him. I couldn't stay that late as I had other obligations. So, what happened? Well…

MENTORSHIP, NETWORKING, AND SOCIAL NETWORKING   33

- Donavion met some incredible contacts who mentored him for the next four years.
- He returned my clothing to me, dry cleaned (completely unnecessary).
- Brooks Brothers tweeted us back when we told them I lent him some clothing for the day!

But, more importantly, those connections definitely paid off. Here's why…

Donavion graduated from college a semester early, which is both a blessing and a curse. Doing so allows you to get a jump on interviewing, but you also miss your last semester of college. Whomp whomp! Something to take note of is that many firms know that they will hire students for May and June starts (after graduation), so it is also likely that your timing will be off.

Like his meal decisions, Donavion put effort into every decision he made, especially the important ones. So I knew he wouldn't take just any job after graduation, rightfully so. We met a few times after he graduated to help him figure it out. I even tried to hire him in sales at a startup firm I was working with. He gracefully declined (or rather, just stopped talking to me about it and I knew that was his answer).

So, I asked that he be hired at the university I was working at. I had switched universities and asked that he be interviewed with a Vice President who also knew him from his time at our previous employer. We all reasoned that a few years in college admissions, which is essentially sales, would:

- Teach him sales strategy and technique
- Allow him to get a graduate degree for free
- Have a decent work-life balance for him to look for strong brands in his off time

Donavion was excited to work at my new university and even said that he'd take me to lunch as a "thank you." A few months into the job, he asked me to lunch. "This is it," I thought. "Free lunch!"

Donavion and I went across the street and got some Chinese food.

Yes, he agonized over what to get. But he also agonized over some news he had to share with me. Donavion would be leaving the university role I helped him secure after a few short months to work at JP Morgan Chase. Based on his incredible resume, he secured an amazing salary ($70K) and he'd be working literally across the street in the legal department.

I couldn't be mad at Donavion. He'd done exactly what we all said he should do. The timing was terrible; but nobody could fault him for going with a brand like that, a brand we all hoped for him. I bought lunch to celebrate his success. Donavion and I still get together and he still asks for advice, which I love.

So here's a young dude who really gets it. He made genuine connections and cultivated them without an ask. He did it because just having those people around was a good enough reward for him. Then, when it very much counted, he asked them for advice and resources to land him the best options. That's a connection you can't fake on social media. He continued to level up his game and even used diversity and inclusion programs like INROADS to kick butt. He learned this from a combination of his family, our program, myself (brushes shoulders off), and the Dean of our school, my boss.

I've met so many incredible networkers in my life. One such networker is a man by the name of Greg Wagner. You'll see a few notes from him throughout this book as he's an admissions KING. Greg can transform any room into an appropriate party. He makes connections, but he also KEEPS connections. He doesn't just make a connection, run away, and never speak to someone again. And he never uses folks. Greg Wagner is probably one of the only folks I know who can outsell me. This stems from his years as an agent, politician, and salesperson. Let's see how he does it.

Wagner begins the conversation. That's the biggest first step. I am a master extrovert, networker, and salesperson, and I often have a hard time starting a conversation. I am super shy at first. Wagner is fearless. He's fearless because of what he does next.

Wagner never asks for a favor. He serves first and for a long time. He'll bring you business. He'll connect you with someone. Sometimes he's just a genuine friend. He is so good at making people feel comfortable because he cares about them. It's not an act.

You'll go years knowing Wagner, and he'll never ask you for anything but the same time and energy he gives you. That's just what he does. A natural connector and extrovert, that's what he's all about. Then, eventually, there may be an opportunity for you to benefit your business by working with him. He'll let you know. If you can, great…If you can't…totally fine. The truth is that most folks like doing for Greg because he does for them. He's caring, kind, and he is so likable. And, he doesn't put pressure on you. So you want to make something work with him. It's that simple!

You've got two very different folks to model after in this chapter: Donavion, who is selective, and Greg, who can throw a slumber party with all of his connections. Which is the best way to be? The answer is "neither." The answer is you should have circles of folks you can connect with and you also MUST have your Personal Advisory Board for contacts, decision making, and general help.

What's a "Personal Advisory Board?" This is something that was given to me by a friend and mentor who worked on Wall Street for years. He told me that I needed to select three folks in my life who were where I wanted to be at some point. I chose him, my brother, and my mentor and boss. All three were chosen for different reasons: family life, wealth, career ambitions, etc.

We developed a verbal (and you can even do a written) contract. The contract stated that when I had a circumstance I needed advice on, they'd be available within 24 hours (or be able to get back to me within 24 hours with a time that worked) to discuss it. They'd provide contacts if needed, advice, and a sounding board. And, in turn, I agreed to take them seriously and only utilize that contract when I really needed it (not deciding on lunch or something stupid).

So what qualifies?

Marriage
Divorce
Starting a business
Changing jobs

Buying a home
Applying for a promotion
Career or life crisis
Etc.

Notice how we select three people. That should tell you how strong your circle is. You don't put everyone in your Personal Advisory Board. This is a gift and a privilege. It's an honor, so start thinking about it. Remember that as your life changes, you can replace folks. No contract voiding is needed. Just let them go. There's good reason for the change. No conflict necessary.

FROM THE EXPERTS

1. 18 percent of social media users can't go beyond "a few hours" without checking Facebook, and 61 percent of users check their newsfeed "at least once a day." - As Reported by Inc.com, a report by TotalDUI (a non-profit out of the University of Maryland). The same article discussed the emergence of "Social Media Rehab" programs. These programs have risen in popularity, consistently, since 2016.

2. More than 70 percent of people land jobs through actual networking. - *US News* estimates. On the other side of that report, it was found that 85 percent of most firm's roles were not filled by online postings.

3. Only 11% of LinkedIn users have more than 100 people in their network - Hubspot, 2017

What's the moral of the story? Build a small online presence, have some fun. But genuine face-to-face connections are part of an art we all need to do a better job at mastering.

PROFESSOR'S PRO TIP

Not having social networking and social media accounts is a terrible idea. People think by staying off of social media, you won't have a narrative. But here are a few things to note:

- Everyone is on social media. Colleges, jobs, clients will wonder why you're not and assume the worst.
- If someone shares something off-color about you (a photo of you in a toga or something worse), it'll be the only thing on the web.
- Folks with your name? You don't want them showing up when someone searches for you.
- Lastly, you get to create a narrative about your life. And you can use any platform from Facebook to Linked In to Tumblr to Blogspot.

Use the chart on the following pages to create your own Personal Advisory Board.

Worksheet: Building Your Personal Advisory Board

1. Select person 1.

   _____

2. List the reasons why.

   _____
   _____
   _____
   _____
   _____
   _____

3. What industry are they in?

   _____

4. What would you like to model?

   _____
   _____

5. Set a time to chat.

   _____

6. Summarize your insights from this chat. Tell them of the verbal contact.

   _____

MENTORSHIP, NETWORKING, AND SOCIAL NETWORKING

1. Select person 2.

_____

    2. List the reasons why.

_____
_____
_____
_____
_____
_____

    3. What industry are they in?

_____

    4. What would you like to model?

_____
_____

    5. Set a time to chat.

_____

    6. Summarize your insights from this chat. Tell them of the verbal contact.

_____

THE COLLEGE ADMISSION

1. Select person 3.

   _____

   2. List the reasons why.

   _____
   _____
   _____
   _____
   _____
   _____

   3. What industry are they in?

   _____

   4. What would you like to model?

   _____
   _____

   5. Set a time to chat.

   _____

   6. Summarize your insights from this chat. Tell them of the verbal contact.

   _____

1. Select person 4.

_____

   2. List the reasons why.

   _____
   _____
   _____
   _____
   _____
   _____
   _____

   3. What industry are they in?

   _____

   4. What would you like to model?

   _____
   _____

   5. Set a time to chat.

   _____

   6. Summarize your insights from this chat. Tell them of the verbal contact.

   _____

CHAPTER 4
SELECTING YOUR CAREER THEN YOUR MAJOR

Okay, I am about to say some contradicting things in this chapter. And, that's okay…first, because you already bought the book so now you need to see the value. You can't return it. Secondly, multiple things can be true at the same time. Once you're equipped with the knowledge that I am going to give you in this chapter, it's your job to decipher what works for you and during what situations.

I have multiple mentors who continue to repeat "Beginning with the end in the mind" as being the first rule to selecting your path. It's paraphrased and quoted from the "2nd Habit" of Franklin Covey's training program called *The 7 Habits of Highly Effective People*. If you haven't gone through their training, I highly suggest it. Or read in its entirety Stephen R. Covey's book, also entitled *The 7 Habits of Highly Effective People*. I think they've added an 8th habit, but I'll always remember the 7.

What does "beginning with the end in mind" mean? I have also used this quote in other chapters in this book, so you'll see it often. It means that we don't just begin something because it looks cool. We begin something because we understand that there is a goal. It's the same reason that I told you to select your Personal Advisory Board of folks who have been where you want to be. Do you think that was a mistake? We need to start thinking about the end of our road so that we know which road to embark on! And yes, we can select the wrong road (as discussed in our introduction). But even if that happens, we'll transfer roads, transfer skills, and move to where we need to go.

So, then you're going to ask me, "Christopher, if you are telling me to select a career to base my major on and that it may be the wrong choice…how do I choose?"

You choose because you have to choose something. And whatever you choose will set you up for success as long as it builds:

- Specific skills
- Transferable knowledge
- Genuine passion
- Competency

Those skills will bring you through multiple jobs. You may wind up doing a very similar thing in every role. You may wind up changing it up a bit. But the bottom line is you need a starting point. And you won't know what that starting point is until you start looking at ending points.

One of the most intelligent young men I've ever met is Angel Cespedes. Angel came to us with tons of integrity and ambition but little knowledge of what major to select or what he was capable of.

"In high school, I became heavily involved in student government and took part in a life-changing program called Virtual Enterprise. The program gave me the opportunity to sharpen my public speaking skills, dress sharp & somewhat understand the concepts of business. My class quickly excelled in the program and our virtual company performed very well for its first year of business competitions. I was fortunate to gain the attention of [Virtual Enterprise] and school leadership who ultimately acquired for me…an interview with an up and coming business program at Mercy College. At this time, I was already shopping around for other colleges and pursuing other unrelated careers such as Graphic Design & Engineering; but for some reason,

Business & Entrepreneurship called out to me, and I took the leap of faith at Mercy."

Now, remember that...Cespedes wanted to be in Graphic Design, right? This is a kid who was super bright but moved from the Dominican Republic at age eight to Harlem / Washington Heights. He had a tough upbringing, so it's safe to say that he didn't have a ton of guidance in the area of academics...until he became the Salutatorian of his high school...that's the second-ranked GPA / Student in the school. He wanted to work as an entrepreneur, and the many business owners you'll speak to say they pay two folks very much money: accountants and lawyers.

"I selected my major, not necessarily because it was fun or always interesting but because it gave me the most value for what I expected to lie ahead. I developed this understanding of the future by asking a lot of questions and listening to my mentors at the time. I was somewhat undecided the first year and ultimately selected Public Accounting. I knew that with Accounting, I would be studying the language of business and develop an understanding of financial statements. The Major allowed me to understand both the technical items and financial concepts. I ultimately leveraged this hard skill with my charisma and critical thinking."

Isn't this dude brilliant? He goes on to say that his end goal is to run his own successful businesses that can add value to society.

"I've already started and I'm using everything I've learned along my journey to my advantage. I've always been an entrepreneur at heart and enjoy the concept of building and growth."

This is the perfect end goal for someone who tells me that his end goal is to leave an environment better than he found it.

And talk about charisma. I can't tell you how many times Cespedes had me rolling on the floor laughing, just by being himself. When once asked how he handles the drama of a very tightly knit, small, and "cliquey" Honors Program, he said, "You know what I'm saying, I'm from Harlem...these girls don't scare me."

Did he really just say that? I loved it!

Cespedes is now past year three of working in Corporate Finance at Via Transportation, a world leader in Transit Tech. He has a vast amount of responsibility and is excited for all the new things to come as his company continues to grow. This was after a quick start in the Big Four as an accountant.

"I've played a substantial role in what Via has become today, and it has been a rewarding journey so far. While I grow at Via, I am simultaneously working on my own ideas and projects that I am nurturing each day and I will pursue full time, someday. On a personal level, I am blessed. I believe the decisions I've made have given me the opportunity to take care of myself and my family."

And what does he say about his major?

"My major was very helpful because it gave me the opportunity to be in the right environments. My career experiences so far have groomed most importantly my mindset and technical knowledge. For example, working in the Big Four was a high-pressure environment with tight deadlines and constant challenges. I was able to quickly learn companies in and out, as well as understand what things need to look like from a financial statement's perspective."

Now, that's one side of a very successful coin. The other side is not so pleasant. I can't tell you how many colleagues, friends, and students come to me without direction. I've had this conversation with so many current students, graduates, and even folks mid-career. The conversations range from:

"What do I do with this major?"
~ to ~
"Nobody told me I wouldn't find a job with this degree."

I am sorry. What? Nobody told you that a degree in art history may not land you a job? Do you know how careers work? You need to begin with the career and then pick the major. If you told me you wanted to be a museum curator, then I'd say "Hey, that's probably a darn good major!"

Now, I've also had conversations with folks who are mid-career who say "I still don't know what I want to be when I grow up." And, that's totally okay. They've likely worked in a field for X amount of years, made some changes, and realized that they are not done finding their passion. But, HOPEFULLY, they are doing this from a place of comfort, where they have the ability to change things up. You want to make enough money where you can say, "Okay, I can't do nothing. But I can do anything." This is challenging, for sure. But, it's not impossible.

And it's absolutely not your college or university's job to select your major for you. But it is their job to figure things out with you. There should be a Career Services Department that assists you in your search. There are some colleges and universities that misrepresent their career services numbers. They will say that 95% of their graduates find employment in their field when all that happened was they got a $2 an hour raise at their job in retail. That's not helpful. Look, if you wanted to work in retail and got a degree in fashion or retail management, I get it. But, that's not what's happening.

I once interviewed for a private art college in New York City that wanted me to be their head of enrollment. VP? Director? I can't remember. But we wound up not seeing eye to eye. Let me break down that conversation for you.

"I'd really like to see the organizational chart," I said to the interview team after my first or second interview.

"That's reasonable," they said.

"Yes," I said. "I want to see what kind of resources I have to recruit students."

"We totally get that," they replied. And they handed me the organizational chart.

"Okay, great," I said. "I'd also like to partner with Marketing and, if possible, I'd really like Career Services to answer to me, too. I can see where students are being placed and also help them find roles and organizations to work with while I am out and about."

"Oh," they clambered. "We don't have a Career Services Department."

"I'm sorry?" I asked. "You don't have what?"

"No, we don't have a Career Services Department."

"So…how do you expect students to find a job after they get their art degree?" I asked.

Well, they put on their 'customer service caps' and answered. "Students come to us for lots of reasons. They may want to work in art, be an art teacher, or even just improve their knowledge of the world of art."

And that's where the conversation ended. I politely excused myself from the interview and told them we wouldn't be a great fit. You can't tell me that there aren't several students in your student body who spend $55,000+ per year to actually get a job. And not catering to those folks is an absolute sin. It's unethical and should have been illegal!

Figuring out your career can be a challenge. You look at someone like Angel Cespedes who did a complete 180-degree turn because he knew his Accounting degree would be a great asset as an entrepreneur. Then there are the folks with Art History or Modern Theater degrees not realizing they can't find a job…because they didn't actually select a major based on their career needs. They selected a major based on their interests. Hey, there's nothing wrong with finding something you're interested in. Like the art school, it's totally possible that folks select a major they want to love and be passionate about. But it's also possible that they want a damn job!

If you want a job, don't wait for someone to tell you what your major does for a living. We've talked about the Personal Advisory Board, looking at data about career services, beginning with the end in mind…all of that jazz. Don't disable yourself by selecting a major and THEN thinking about your career. Just be smart.

And don't select something broad because you think that it'll give you more options. It will not. English, Psychology, History, Mathematics, etc. They are not going to be helpful without specializations, internships and extra-curriculars.

Hey, I've been there. I selected the Major of Psychology at Siena College and came in with lots of Psych credits. I continued with that Major until I realized I wanted to do other stuff. So what did I do? I picked up specializations in Business, Writing, and Communications. Easy enough! I also interned and worked in radio, television, the music business, sales/marketing, and e-commerce. So things worked out pretty okay. But, I had SO many interests and SO many "ends in mind" that I didn't know which "end" I wanted.

But it seemed to have worked out. I was able to bring my transferable skills into any of my fields. And when I saw "new ends" that I wanted to get to, I started new beginnings.

One such occurrence happened when I finished my MBA. I had gotten my MBA to be successful in business. I never wanted to be an educator. That wasn't because I didn't feel education was important or because I found education to be a skill set I was incapable of acquiring. I actually thought I'd be a great teacher and went into fields like training, HR, and consulting which are educational in nature. In fact, the way I sell is educational.

No, it was that I felt teachers were all on an even playing field. And the better teachers didn't make better pay. Furthermore, there was a stigma in my head that told me that great teachers were not great "doers" despite some incredible teachers I'd had in my life.

So then why, when I finished my MBA and had lunch with my manager at Yahoo! Inc., did I reply the way I was about to?

"Christopher," Mr. Woodard (aka "Woody") asked. "What do you want to do now that you have your MBA?"

"Well," I told him. "I am so envious of my professors. I think that's who I want to be like."

It was true, I saw my college professors like rock stars, informing me of best practices and showing me the ropes in business. That's who I wanted to be...on stage and helping others be successful like me. I'd already worked for a Fortune 500 brand. I'd reached the Director level. I owned my own home, earned an incredible salary, and could do anything I wanted to!

"Well," Woody said to me, "Do you see where there is a problem?"

I was confused.

"You should have said you wanted to be like me."

Now, Woody was NOT and is not an egotist. He didn't care what I wanted to do as long as I was happy. An older manager, he'd gotten his career started at Yahoo! Inc. a bit later than the rest of us. He owned a successful catering company prior to that but needed to take a step back after his stress-induced heart condition caused some serious health risks. He was no stranger to making career changes mid-swing!

"Let's put you in a position to be successful," Woody said, and I was grateful. I enjoyed sales, marketing, training, and HR but I really wanted to be an educator now that I'd seen how much fun they had and how impactful they could be.

So, I made some lifestyle changes:

- I took on more consulting jobs to increase my income and decrease time spent in the office.
- I started researching Ph.D.s
- I began adjuncting so that I could get experience.

And within a few years, I was a full-time college professor and Program Director. Then Assistant Dean, Honors Director, Professor in Residence, and finally...Dean. My transferable skills in sales and marketing helped me build programs. My love for HR helped me find new professors. My excellence in training made me a great teacher. And that's the end I am most comfortable with.

FROM THE EXPERTS

1. 19.5% of college graduates earning Bachelor's Degrees major in business; 12.4% major in healthcare and related programs while 8.1% major in social sciences and history. 23.4% of graduates earning Master's Degrees major in business; 17.8% major in education while 15.3% major in healthcare. - Educationdata.org

2. The 10 majors with the lowest median earnings are: early childhood education ($39,000); human services and community organization ($41,000); studio arts, social work, teacher education, and visual and performing arts ($42,000); theology and religious vocations, and elementary education ($43,000); drama and theater arts and family and community service ($45,000). - https://cew.georgetown.edu/cew-reports/valueofcollegemajors/

3. Two of the top highest paying majors, STEM and business, are also the most popular majors, accounting for 46 percent of college graduates. The top-paying college majors earn $3.4 million more than the lowest-paying majors over a lifetime. - https://cew.georgetown.edu/cew-reports/valueofcollegemajors/

PROFESSOR'S PRO TIP

I know nobody likes to hear this, but if you're stuck on a college major, think about things that are in demand. Not many folks want to go into accounting, but they know it's a valuable field to be in. It's the same thing I say about being an entrepreneur…everyone wants to design a new app…but the folks who own your local dry cleaners do much better financially (on average, of course).

You don't know these things. You need to ask questions to folks who are successful. When I was a kid, my dad was a plumber. He was my hero. So I wanted to be a plumber. Do you know how bad of a plumber I'd be? I can barely repair a vase without gluing my fingers together!

Use the worksheet on the following pages to collect salient information from individuals you consider to be successful. Compare and contrast their responses.

Worksheet

I want you to interview folks who have done what you've done. Then you can build a data sheet about their majors. Do something like this:

Hero #1 Name
_____

Career / Field of Choice
_____

Income Level
_____

College Major
_____

Internships in College
_____

Hero #2 Name
_____

Career / Field of Choice
_____

Income Level
_____

College Major
_____

Internships in College
_____

Hero #3 Name
_____

Career / Field of Choice
_____

Income Level
_____

College Major
_____

Internships in College
_____

Hero #4 Name
_____

   Career / Field of Choice
   _____

   Income Level
   _____

   College Major
   _____

   Internships in College
   _____

Hero #5 Name
_____

   Career / Field of Choice
   _____

   Income Level
   _____

   College Major
   _____

   Internships in College
   _____

CHAPTER 5
THE INTERNSHIP PARADIGM

You've seen these memes before:

"We Want our Interns with 10 years of experience, two houses, and a Ph.D."

Right?

Here's the deal: School, if you choose to go that route, is important as hell. Yeah, you need the book stuff. I know it, you know it. That "stuff" teaches you how to think on your feet, be receptive, learn, etc. And depending on the major of choice, you may even learn the technical skills you need during labs, workshops, etc. Yes, all of it is wonderful.

But most of the students I work with will tell me that they have learned more during their internships than they did in four years of college. They have learned technical skills, office etiquette, how to network, and the adult life of waking up, going to work, etc., etc. Believe it or not, that is super important. But the most important thing that an internship does is show a future employer that you have the drive, ambition and the ability to pair your academics with real-world experience and keep progressing. It's a right of passage that every company wants to see. And if you're lucky, although it doesn't happen often, your internship could lead you directly to a job at that firm. Yes, getting a four-year degree is valuable and without being enrolled in school, you won't get the internship. Without the internship, you won't get the job.

Nobody made this more clear than Andrew Vatier. Andrew Michael Vatier was everything you could want in a first-year student: intelligent, charismatic, willing, and able. He came to our small private college and honors program, not because we were the strongest, academically. In fact, at the time, there was nothing that would endorse us in writing as a strong academic institution. Vatier connected with the people and professors who were just like him: smart enough, charismatic, good communicators, and they used real experience in the classroom. But the one thing that really drew him to our department was the ability to use connections to get him an internship.

Vatier will never tell you this about himself, but he is a genius. And I don't mean he's a Mensa level 1600 SAT 200 IQ kid who spent his time with his nose in a book. Quite the opposite, actually. Vatier was the student body president in high school. He was always surrounded by friends, but his most valued companion was his grandfather, from whom he said he learned a great deal. I don't care who you are or what you can google, when you are 17 and have the patience to look away from your laptop and spend time with an elderly family member, you're brilliant. Because the things you'll learn in those conversations trump anything a hashtag will show you. And, I think, because of those conversations, he was also a 40-year-old in a 17-year-old's body. Very wise.

Vatier was also a stand-up comedian. I don't mean he was a funny guy. I mean that for the better part of his teens, Vatier actually got paid to do stand-up comedy. This is not someone without options. So I remember the funny conversations I'd had with Vatier when he sat in my office and said things like, "Look, I didn't come here because you have the best reputation. You're not Harvard. I came here because I know you'll get me an internship."

Vatier put his faith in one of our more senior faculty members who got him his first internship at Dow Jones. That same summer, he also interned at UBS Financial Services. Yes, read that again. He interned at two different places in one summer. I remember him telling me that the few weeks at Dow Jones were cool because he was in the hot seat, lending his millennial expertise to an older brand that was trying to figure out how to get the *Wall Street Journal* into young people's hands. Meanwhile, his internship at UBS was much more traditional: making copies, doing clerical work, etc. Neither was better or worse. I think lots of students go into an internship thinking, "Why aren't they asking me for my opinion?" The reality is that you don't really know much as a 17-year-old. I'm sorry to say it. The best wisdom comes from successes. And the best successes come from failures. You haven't had enough failures yet to be a success. Yes, we can get into the .0001% of college students who drop out with a great startup. If that's who you are, I'll give you my email address because I want to be on your board of directors with stock options. But when the situation arises to give your opinion as a young person, that is an incredibly fun internship.

Vatier describes internships as a "sandbox where you can learn all these skills without a chance for major error." He had four distinct internships during his four years in college including Dow Jones, UBS Financial Services, CIBC (Canadian Imperial Bank of Commerce), and JP Morgan Chase. I loved listening to his successes and learning how his mentors praised him. During those internships, Vatier really built skills, learned what he liked and didn't like, and I saw a huge amount of growth in him with every single summer that passed. He really took the most out of those internships.

But he didn't have to and, in fact, most students don't. Just "showing up" is something he discussed being half the battle. Wearing your suit or work clothes, waking up, doing "adult-like" activities, operating in an office, etc. Success is "caught, not taught." So being present during your internship is huge. Vatier met tons of mentors who genuinely wanted to pass down their knowledge to him, and he was eager to ask what he could do to help them. He told me a wonderful story.

"When I was interning at CIBC my direct boss was the CRO (Chief Risk Officer) in the Americas. He had his own corner office as I sat out on the floor in my cubical. One morning, he walked by my desk and said 'I didn't know you were here yet; say "Good Morning" when you come in, everyone likes a good morning check.' To this day, when I get to my desk, I ensure to go out of my way to say, 'Good Morning,' to my boss & team. Even on those dark Mondays where you can hear a pin drop in the office, a 'Good Morning' is a friendly way to say 'I am here, good to see you, I am ready to get our day going.' It still amazes me how far a consistent friendly morning greeting can go a long way in how your team, boss, and company view you as a member of their organization."

Vatier graduated from Mercy College in 2016 and is now at Bloomberg LP.

"My experience in internships," he says, "has been the catalyst for any success I have had early in my career. The skills of being in an office setting, answering to a senior boss, completing tasks while managing expectations, and playing a role on a team or in an organization are expected when you graduate."

This is the kind of dude you want to be like. Intelligent enough to know he doesn't know everything…unlike some people I know very well. Let me tell you about a professional I know better than anyone.

There was a young student at Siena College, my alma mater, who wanted to make a name for himself. So he started to fill up his resume as much as he could. First of all, let's dissect this kid:

1. He wanted to get attention from his resume, not jobs.
2. He started filling it up as opposed to learning skills.

This kid was going about things all wrong. By the time he graduated, he was the head or founder of over 15 different clubs and organizations from the campus radio station to the comic book club to the literary magazine. He was in student government, had a major and two minors, and his internships? Sheesh! Let me tell you something.

This guy had so many different internships:

- He interned for J-Records one year.
- He interned for Island 94.3 Radio
- He interned for the *Times Union* newspaper
- He worked for Clearchannel Broadcasting and a few other radio stations

- He worked for a small Contracting Company
- He worked for an E-Commerce Brand

This is all great. Trust me, we love diversity. Try things out until you figure out what you like. But this guy was trying too many things. And at the end of his four years in school, he didn't know what he wanted to do! Work in radio? Business? Write for a newspaper? Be an entrepreneur?

By now, you've probably figured out that the kid is me. I would never be this hard on someone else. You're all welcome to make some mistakes. Let me tell you one or two of mine during the internship process. And they all stem from one thing: I enjoyed achieving things more than doing them. There's a great book I'm not going to get into called *Growth Mindset*. The basic premise: Some people like to learn skills and some people like to earn trophies. Is there more to it? Absolutely. I'm not going to say that's the entire book. But in a nutshell, I was way more interested in saying I could do something than actually doing it. It took me over a decade to change that mindset and it hurt! But back then…

I wanted to start getting some internships that really mattered under my belt. There was a guy at the campus radio station I was DJing at who skyrocketed into a leadership role because he interned the summer of his freshman year. And I was so mad that I didn't get a solid radio internship that summer that I just started applying like crazy. But then I thought to myself, *What if I got a really great internship for a talk show host? I'd learn the ins and outs of show business and everything in between. People would have no choice but to say I'm awesome and give me a leadership role next year.* Sigh…so much wrong with this statement. But I did think it.

There was one major problem: I was way too late to apply to those internships. They were already full. I had applied to others I was waiting on. But I had a mentor who kind of sort of knew David Letterman (like David didn't know him, but he knew David kind of thing). He told me that if I got David's attention, I'd have a shot at getting into a last-minute internship. So, here's what I did:

I created a DVD of the "Top 10 Reasons You Should Hire Me," and then I made these ridiculous short clips contradicting them. Like, "I'm a good dresser" was said while I was wearing pajamas, and "People like me!" was said with my roommates shaking their head "no" in the background. I sent it to *The David Letterman Show* in a huge envelope with stickers and hearts drawn on it. And sure enough, I did get a call from David Letterman's people saying they'd sneak me in as an intern!

But there was a conundrum! I had already accepted an internship offer at J-Records which I felt I had to take. The moral of the story was that if I really wanted to take the better-branded internship, I could have. But I think in my brain, I just wanted to say that I got it. Gross!

So I went through my few internships and jobs and started building my resume from there. I did get a leadership position at the radio station. I joined student government. I went through "all of the motions" of building my resume and accumulating "stuff" just to say I could do them. I didn't actually make conscious efforts to learn what I liked and didn't like about the jobs and internships I had, mostly because I was lazy and felt that just showing up was all I needed to do. Showing up is half of what you need to. Actually doing "the stuff" is very important. Or at least being eager enough to want to do those things works!

During my senior year, I had one final internship. I needed an internship in writing to fulfill my internship class for my writing minor. I'm sure there was an alternative, but it was probably more fun to find and take an internship! So, through the campus career center and some hard work, I found an internship with the *Times Union*, a local Albany newspaper. I secured it, used it for my class, and all was well!

Well, so it seemed. The man who ran the internship class was Dr. Leslie, an "odd duck" kind of writing professor who wrote an entire poetry book about different types of plants (or was it cacti?) Either way, he was a unique character. Dr. Leslie changed the way I wrote poetry, for the better, in one of my poetry classes. And he challenged everything I thought I knew in one of my short story classes. But he was also one of those guys with whom you didn't really know if you stood in a good place. He was dry and quirky. Unfortunately, he died a few years back, and the entire Siena community was saddened. He changed a lot of lives, including mine.

By the end of the semester, and with my internship completely done, I received my grade from Dr. Leslie. He gave me a B+ in the internship class. Really? B+? This was a damn "bird" course! You fly through it! You just show up, talk about your internship in your group, and leave! Why on earth did he give me a B+? This went back to my previous statement. As brilliant as this dude was, you didn't know where you stood with him! I decided to approach him in his office.

"Look, Dr. Leslie," I said. "I don't know why you don't like me, but I don't deserve a B+ in this class. I did every assignment and went to every session." I knew he was trouble.

"Well," Dr. Leslie grumbled, barely opening his mouth as he did. "I actually do like you..." And at that moment, I could feel the previous two classes we took together coming to fruition. He was hard on me because he liked me. Okay, I can buy that.

"So, then why did you decide to decrease my grade to a B+ in this class?" I asked, assuming any internship supervisor would just give me an A because they didn't care - and I was awesome.

"Well," he said. "I didn't. Your internship supervisor felt you should have received a C in this class. He said you wrote far fewer articles than any other intern he's had. And you didn't show hustle or seem to ask for more work. I took it upon myself, knowing you're an exemplary student and a decent writer, to increase your grade to a B+. You did, in fact, do all of the work in my class."

As he was saying this, I began to look back at all of the internships and jobs I'd held throughout my four years of college. The frustration supervisors had with me when I was lazy. The number of times I was happy just getting the job done versus doing it well or helping others. I remember a supervisor rolling his eyes at me at an internship and thinking, "They don't know what they are thinking!"

The reality is that I was far better at getting the trophy than doing the actual thing I needed to do to keep the trophy. And I didn't really care to figure it all out. Wowza! What an eye-opener!

Looks like you schooled me in a third writing class, Dr. Leslie...

So, what could I do to fix it?

The first thing I did was really understand that I was completely trophy-hungry and arrogant. That's a hard realization. Secondly, I had to actually develop some skills so that I could turn my lack of learning during my internships into a solid career. And lastly, I had to completely redo any networking I had already done because I probably introduced a lot of people to the wrong version of myself.

But all problems can be fixed with some hard work and integrity, yes? I spent the first few years of my career in sales and business development, while I earned my MBA. (Did I mention that a BA in Psychology is about as useful as an air conditioner in an ice storm?) While selling products, I learned some very specific skills, mostly related to what I was selling:

- E-Commerce Products
- Digital Advertising
- Search Engine Optimization (SEO) and Pay Per Click (PPC)
- Graphics
- Social Media
- Data Uploads for large selling platforms

It wasn't until I became proficient in these ideas that I could sell them, train on them, manage people who sold them, etc. I even consulted in the digital world!

Then, as I became an educator, I earned my Ph.D. I learned quickly that skills in market research and statistics were much more valuable than anything I'd picked up already. But I was able to combine it all into the educator and business person I am today.

Doing for the sake of learning also guided me in the right direction as far as networking goes. I was able to join non-profit organizations' workgroups and committees…anything to help me use my skills to meet people and be of use to others. Within the first ten years of my career, I was very well networked both on Long Island and in certain industries in New York City, specifically because I donated my time and energy (as well as skills) to others. It had nothing to do with winning the trophy or adding letters to my name. It was genuine networking with the desire to help and yielded a group of great colleagues who were willing to help me when the time was ever right and they could spare the energy.

PROFESSOR'S PRO TIP

It's never too early to start interning. Honestly…it's literally never too early. But before you just jump into the internship pool, you may want to start thinking about where to focus your energy. An internship doesn't actually mean it's going to be helpful. Interning at your local pizzeria when you have no intention of working in food services won't likely be helpful. I'd rather a potential Accounting hire go through a two-week leadership program in accounting at their school than intern in social media at a fashion brand. So yes…the short answer is that you should be interning as early as your first year in college (some even do one during their senior year in high school… which can be considered excessive or useful, or both). And doing something is better than nothing. But don't just spin your wheels. Be strategic in whatever you do.

It's ridiculously important to work backward. This requires thinking about potential end games/goals. What jobs would you want when you graduate? Realistically, that is. Then, ask some mentors and professors/teachers what they think would be ideal stepping stones. Google the hell out of those jobs and search Linked-In and other tools to see their competitors, companies, and positions like the ones you want. Then, find some version of those positions so that you can start inching your way up. A focused summer is way more valuable than one with a baseless internship that won't get you the job.

FROM THE EXPERTS

1. A study from the National Association of Colleges and Employers found that paid internships turn into official job offers about 65 percent of the time. Unpaid internships produce job offers 39 percent of the time. (https://www.naceweb.org/

job-market/internships/the-impact-of-unpaid-internships-on-career-development/)

2. That same study tells us that in recent years about 1.5 million internships are filled in the United States annually. That means less than 10 percent of college grads get to do an internship. THAT'S Important to note.

3. From NACE by way of CollegeRecruiter.com, the students who completed at least one internship prior to graduation were way more likely to receive multiple job offers for positions after graduation. For those who completed at least one internship, the average student received 1.17 job offers. Those without an internship received 16 percent fewer job offers, less than one job offer per student. (https://www.collegerecruiter.com/blog/2019/09/30/how-internships-impact-employability-and-salary/)

PROFESSOR'S PRO TIP

Want an internship? Cheat! What do I mean? Don't wait until you are an eligible junior. Find an internship as early as your first year of college…maybe even the summer of! I don't care if it's with "Joe's Deli" and you're building their social media accounts. Just do it. Unpaid, if you have to. Get something on your resume so that when you WANT the big internship, you have shown a history of progressive steps forward. If you can't find an internship, volunteer somewhere. Trust me, it makes a difference.

WORKSHEET

You should be keeping track of your internship efforts. The majority of my students applied to at least ten internships before they found the one that fit them.

Use the chart below to track your internships.

Position	Status (Started, Completed, Waiting on Parts)	Application Due Date	Decision Date	Correspondence	Notes	Interview Date

CHAPTER 6
MINDFULNESS AND DIET

"Oh, who is in the bathroom?" someone asked at MMA.

"Oh, you know…that girl…the one who lost 30 pounds."

What? You don't know her name, but you know she lost 30 pounds?

"You'd better get on the mat and roll…instead of having rolls," said to a young girl during jiu-jitsu practice.

"Yeah…it's great that you're starting young. I wish I started younger." Grabs belly. A young man talking to a younger kid at the gym during personal training sessions.

These are things both overheard and said directly to me in what I thought were some of the most welcoming communities I belong to: the gym, martial arts classes, training sessions, etc. We grunt. We spit. We sweat. We kick each other in the face! How do we speak about each other and ourselves this way when we're together? Absolutely awful.

Look, I love being healthy. I eat well… (okay that's kind of a lie). I work out a lot, meditate, journal, etc. I do try to get to the doctor for my heart (I had open-heart surgery when I was 30) and for other reasons. Men typically don't go to the doctor, BUT I make it a point to get a check-up in blood work, heart work, even STI checks (uh.... yeah...when you become active, you should do it. It's like your bank account. Not looking there doesn't mean it ain't overdrawn). But I would NEVER comment on my own or someone else's body like that. And this is coming from a man who has body dysmorphia.

So how do we remain healthy while building our careers? There are tons of books on this. Lots of products. I am not going to bore you with all of the things you've already heard. What I will say is that I have learned quite a bit from both former students/young folk and my mentors and coaches who have been successful before me. I shall discuss them both.

Did you know that large investment banks like Goldman Sachs had to tell their interns not to work more than 17 hours per day and sleep at the office? (https://www.businessinsider.com/r-goldman-to-summer-interns-dont-stay-in-the-office-overnight-2015-6) In the 80s and 90s, there were rumors that these banks gave out awards for "most nights spent sleeping at the office." So this is a good transition away from that level of craziness. I, myself, am a workaholic, so it's very likely I would have fallen into that culture.

Why do we value this "workaholic" attitude? I cannot tell you how often I am praised for my "work ethic." The truth is, it's a terrible way to live. The "work hard/play hard" mentality is simply not sustainable for a long period of time. I'd rather adopt the "work focused and rest properly" mentality. Let's discuss a few folks who have done it right.

I have encountered numerous young folks (students, mostly) who have taken the time to meditate, read, journal, eat properly, etc. This is a FAR CRY from how I spent my time in college. Here was my general routine:

- Wake up with just enough time to get to class (skipping breakfast or grabbing something VERY fast at the dining hall)
- Going to class half asleep (I didn't drink coffee until after college—I should have never started)
- Grab lunch either to go or at the dining hall.
- Sit in the "Leadership Lounge" between classes to relax with

my friends, discuss various clubs and organizations we were involved in
- Record my radio or television shows
- Go to work
- Eat dinner somewhere in between
- Hit the gym a few times a week
- Stay up late finishing homework
- Rinse and repeat

Let's not forget the Thursdays, Fridays, and Saturdays of drinking and partying. My favorite time to think about was when I was on "Weight Watchers." I started it my junior year and was on and off for the next few years. I now prefer intuitive eating. But, moreover, I was restricted to a certain amount of "points."

I can promise you, this is not at all the path to success. It worked out fine for me. However, looking back, I could have been a far better student leader with:

- Proper rest
- Early mornings
- Less drinking (and late nights)
- Fewer friends (yes, that's a thing)

I am about to sound very old for a moment. We had very few social media sites (not apps) when I was in college. Facebook didn't hit my campus until my senior year. (I actually wrote an article about it in our school newspaper.) Smartphones weren't a thing. I had a flip phone with a keyboard that was pretty dope.

But trust me when I tell you... no matter what...you'll find a distraction if you want one. Socrates and his crew used to say that kids read too many books. Yes...they READ TOO MUCH. Because that was the only form of entertainment. For me, it was MySpace and there were a few other sites that connected folks: Hot or Not...I can't remember the rest. AOL chat...yeah...I'm old. I'd stay up half the night connecting with people I didn't know. Go out to party, hang out with friends and girls (I had a girlfriend for most of my time in college, thank goodness…at least it was just ONE girl). But, man…let me tell you something:

YOU DON'T NEED TO BE EVERYWHERE AND HANG OUT WITH EVERYONE. You are not missing anything.

Isolation is fine. Working and learning are COOL. Who are the folks you idolize? Elon Musk? Jeff Bezos? Even actors like Robert Downey, Jr.? Singers like Lizzo? Kamala Harris? Do you think those folks sit on their phones all day and talk to people? Do they get fast food and smoke a bowl on a Tuesday afternoon? Binge drink four days a week? No! Even in college, they didn't do that! Elon Musk was notorious for renting his house out as a nightclub. Was he partying? Maybe…but not as much as he was making money! I had a manager once who told me all about how he made money in college. He bought some old beat-up buses, got his license to drive them, and brought his classmates to and from the bar on weekends. I am sure he didn't have time to drink in between runs!

These folks are regimented:

- Early wake up
- Self-reflection, meditation/prayer
- Maybe reading
- Something physical
- Healthy breakfast
- Start working
- Breaks throughout the day
- Healthy lunch or early dinner
- Maybe the gym and then time with family or alone, relaxing
- Prep for the next day (meal prep, coffee, set alarms, etc.)
- Early to bed
- Rinse and repeat

There are different versions of this, of course. Some folks go to networking events at night. Others take lunch with clients. Life isn't always going to be balanced. One of my mentors used to always make sure our students knew that. You can't have a perfectly balanced day, every day. In fact, sometimes, an entire decade won't be balanced. But, over the course of your life, you MUST keep your balance. You want to work your tail off in your 20s? Great idea. Use that energy. Then you can chill in your 50s. But try to reverse it and you'll wind up working two jobs so you can pay for dog food. No bueno.

So how do you balance? How do you practice self-care? There are a few folks in my life who've taught me great balance and high productivity. The human body is a machine. We don't let it run properly when we mistreat it or neglect the things it needs.

While I was earning my MBA, I had two mentors who really understood their bodies well. One was the Dean of my Business School who was one of the most productive people I've ever met. One thing she did (that I think very much helped her) was skipping a big lunch because she felt it slowed her down throughout the day. We didn't get into a conversation about it, but I have to assume she had a nice big breakfast before she began her day.

The second mentor I had during that time was one of my managers at Yahoo! Inc. A former small business owner, his heart doctor told him he needed to take a step back after his heart attack. So he began a new career working for the internet giant in sales. Was it high stress? Sure. But not as high stress as owning his own business. And he thrived like crazy. He was one of the best salespeople and managers I've ever met. He also knew when to take time away from the office, which was really inspired by Yahoo! When our office sales weren't hitting the numbers we needed to hit, he told us to close up shop and go to his country club for lunch and a swim. When 5:00 p.m. hit, he would literally come and stand by your computer until you shut it down. The only way you could stay late is if you had clients on the West Coast to call. When you left early for any reason, the entire team…in fact our floor…clapped you out of the office! That was especially embarrassing when I had to leave for a funeral one day!

These are just two of the many I tap into when I think about my own well-being. As I write this chapter, I am transitioning into joining the "Sunrise Club" which my life coach has helped me join. In fact, I just had a radio show on my dating network the other night discussing the busy lives of entrepreneurs and career-driven folks. Specifically, we were discussing the balance of relationships and work. My guest, Neil

McMullin, owner and founder of the Whimzy App, has an impenetrable schedule. He's a 5 AM-er, like me. But I struggle, as I have only been waking up that early for the past year. So on my show, "The Barbershop," I asked him...

"So, what happens when you go to bed late...you must wake up late those days, right?"

His answer was, "No, mate...I don't. I wake up. At 5:00 a.m. every morning."

That is the reality of what has to happen, I am realizing. You must not waver in your self-care routine. So, what is his routine?

- Up at 5:00 a.m.
- Meditation, journaling, and self-reflection
- Work as much as he can for 12 hours, taking breaks when needed
- Slow down, time with his partner
- Bed early
- Repeat

This is Monday - Friday, no matter what. He goes to bed late? Wakes up at five. Doesn't feel great? Wakes up at five. Had a rough night? Wakes up at five. It is unwavering.

Why do I take these routines so seriously? Because good habits create good feelings and productive behaviors. Bad habits will do the opposite. Think about lots of the incredibly gifted artists you listen to, watch, etc. such as Judy Garland, Kurt Cobain, Heath Ledger, John Belushi...Elvis! These folks were geniuses who disrupted their routines and created unhealthy lifestyles. They pushed their bodies to the limit without thinking of the recourse. It's the same reason I meet dozens and dozens of Wall Street executives who burn out and decide to become high school teachers, professors, stay-at-home parents. Please don't mistake these professions as failures or retreats, or misinterpret my saying that as an implication that one must burn out to consider these things. I became a professor, and I never burned out (well that's debatable!). But what I am saying is that a 100-mile-an-hour lifestyle is just not sustainable. Altering your brain with drugs? Same effect. Not taking care of your body? Same effect.

Look, I know what you're thinking…you go to college to learn about yourself, grow, sign up to Tinder, and party… Yes, that's true. You absolutely want to have some fun while you're in college. It should be the best four years of your life.

BUTTTTTT!

Should the best four years of your life be so much fun that the next forty years kind of suck? The answer is no. You definitely don't want to be old and balding, staring into the abyss of history talking about "the one who got away" or "the good ol' days." My alma mater, Siena College, where I earned my undergraduate degree, has one of my favorite slogans discussing how four years of education will create 40 years of success. Now THAT is the way you should think about college. Yes, have fun! But enjoy yourself in ways OTHER than drinking and promiscuity. Explore:

- Sunrises/sunsets
- A small business out of your dorm
- Hiking
- Intramural Sports
- Auditing a class
- Food tours
- Study abroad/traveling
- All of the etc. you can think of

And, yes, absolutely, cut loose a little bit with your friends, fraternity/sorority folks, or study group. Binge drink on a Friday night so that you remember on Saturday why you shouldn't do that. Stay up all night on a Saturday night doing something ridiculous like seeing which 24-hour convenience store in town has the best snacks. Prank your housemates when they are gone for the weekend by stacking their beds or hiding all of their left sneakers. TOTALLY BUILD MEMORIES. But build good habits, too. Trust me on this one.

I will certainly tell you that some of my funniest memories were during your typical Friday night parties. In fact, I had a student come up to me one day and say, "Hey, I play soccer with someone who went to college with you and he says you're crazy." He then proceeded to tell me about a drunken story that should not have been repeated, whereby I may or may not have defended the honor of a good friend...while on a cruise ship...by potentially pushing someone towards the edge of it... Look...he was physically trying to fight someone. If anything...I was stopping the fight from happening. Right?

But truthfully? My most memorable times had nothing to do with drinks or staying out or trying to kiss a stranger. I can remember vividly the taste of hamburgers and hot dogs at Ted's Fish Fry while my best friend and I were studying for finals. I remember the night we accidentally ran over the hooves of a dead deer about an hour from campus on our way home from visiting a good friend who was in need. We were up until 2:00 a.m. trying to get that damn tire off!

How about the first blizzard we experienced? A bunch of Long Island kids up in the Adirondacks experiencing that much snow for the first time? The weather was a bit different back then. Long Island didn't get the snowfall it does now. It was literally the perfect storm: a blizzard, no classes or finals the next day. (Reading Day was a day we had to study in between classes and finals. This was the night before Reading Day). Some kids were going out. Others stayed in making soup and watching movies while the snow fell. After a while, we were stir crazy. We went outside to make a snowman...and well...one of us got hit with a snowball. And...the rest of the night was in God's hands. The local police had to come to stop the snowball fight. It was hysterical.

As I said, those are the times you'll remember the most. Don't have FOMO while trying to hook up the most, drink the most, smoke the most, whatever. I know you're going to think I sound like a "dad" right now, but good things happen in small doses!

Now, didn't we say something up top about God's hands? Did we talk about spirituality at all during this book? We did not. Let's chat about it.

Look, I am religious. I am also spiritual. I am also a believer in tarot and other psychic-type methods. And here's my thought on all of it: you are connected to the rest of the planet and you are connected to others. For anyone who thinks they are not, just wait. You will feel connected to someone or something at some point that will change your mind. At least, I hope you do. Call it spirituality, faith, religion, karma, etc. It is what it is. Call it what you want. But the energy that you put out into the universe comes back to you. Like, freal freal…

Remember the movie *Avatar*? Not *The Last Airbender*, the other one. The one with the blue giants…

Think about your energy like that movie. They were connected to animals, plants, the planet, and each other. They didn't always have to speak in order to communicate. They were connected and contacted. It was beautiful.

This can be you. Don't be silly. You don't have to call it anything. Just reflect and connect. Think before speaking or doing. Take action deliberately. You know the best path in your gut. And the rest you leave to your advisory board to help you with.

So, before we get into the tips, I thought I'd share some data/information from the Trello blog. A few things they recommend that I completely agree with:

- Eliminate decision making: to me, that means setting your clothes out prior to that day. I have 18 suits. I wear 4. Why do I have 18? I have no idea. Pack your lunch and even make your coffee if you don't mind reheating it. Set your dog's food out if you want.
- Check your calendar so you know what the day will be like. (You can do that the night before, too, in my book.)
- Cuddle a loved one or pet.
- Hydrate…. OMG YES!
- Move around.
- Be gracious and write down what you are thankful for. I literally have post-its next to my bed that I'll write things I am happy about. Most of them are about my ability to write, be a professor/dean, or own my businesses. I write, "You prayed for

this so shut the **** up and do it!" on post-its all over my room and offices.

See more at:
https://blog.trello.com/best-productive-morning-routines

PROFESSOR'S PRO TIP

Be unreasonably rigid about your schedule. One of my absolute favorite colleagues and friends, Wazi, goes to bed way early because he wakes up before 5:00 a.m. (around 4:30) every day. This is not an option. He does not stay out late. He does not drink. He does not eat poorly. He treats his body like a synagogue; and yes, he is a person of faith. Because of this rigidity, I have never seen this man down for very long. He's made millions of dollars and has been at the top of his field (or several) for almost his entire life.

Here's the tip: Don't adjust your schedule. Be flexible elsewhere. Your body gets used to certain patterns. Eat McDonald's every day? It will get used to that. Work out every day? It will crave that. Wake up and get serotonin from Tinder every day? It will want that. See what's going on? Create a pattern that is sustainable and challenging. Mine includes waking up 30 minutes earlier than I want to, walking my dog, Joker, praying, meditating, journaling, and writing before I do ANYTHING. If I have an urge to check my phone, I check my stocks and bitcoin. I don't look at a dating app or on social media unless I must for my business. And do you know what? Once 8:00 a.m. hits, I've gotten all of that done, and anything else I do is gravy and well deserved.

Does that have to be your mantra? Nope! Stay up late if you want. Dedicate time during the afternoon to do these things. Whatever works for you works for you. But seriously— nobody/nothing should get in the way of that pattern because you may resent that activity or person. Moreover, you'll be angry with yourself. Be relentless with your schedule. It's the best way to be successful...and moreover...happy!

STATISTICS

1. A critical review of 17 studies found that religious attendance and intrinsic (internalized) religion tend to be associated with reduced anxiety, while extrinsic (utilitarian) religion tends to be positively associated with anxiety. A meta-analysis of 147 studies concluded that there was a robust but modest inverse association between religiousness and depressive symptoms.

David R Williams and Michelle J Sternthal, Med J Aust 2007; 186 (10): S47. || doi: 10.5694/j.1326-5377.2007.tb01040.x Published online: 21 May 2007

2. 73% of folks interviewed in morningroutine.com use an alarm to wake up. 63% of folks do yoga or meditate. 79% exercise. And 68% of those folks sleep in on weekends.

3. Google how much sleep you need. It's a minimum of seven hours. Maximum nine. While you can make up for sleep within the week, due to some research suggestions, try not to. (nectarsleep.com, healthline.com)

Worksheet

Here's a simple worksheet to help you stay on track throughout your day, with all of the most popular activities you'll want to accomplish before you start your day. Pick and choose which you want to do each day perhaps?

Activity	Monday	Tuesday	Wednesday	Thursday	Friday	Saturday	Sunday
Journaling							
Prayer							
Meditation							
Workout							
Coffee							
Check Stocks							
Light Chores							
Check Plants							
Feed/Walk Pet							
Check on Pet							
Read							
Drink Water							
Quick Shower							
Gratitude Journal							
Hobby							

CHAPTER 7
ACADEMICS

Okay, so maybe you've heard me say a bunch of times that academics are not as important as you think they are, but that doesn't mean they aren't important at all! There are a few things you want to consider when you're thinking about academics:

- Is what I'm about to do academically going to get me to where I need to be, professionally?
- Can I actually do the things expected of me in that academic program?
- Is there a potential link via an alternative route, if that academic program is not something I'll excel in?

The second question might bother you, and I get it. "Well, can't I do anything?" Sure, you can absolutely make anything happen with enough drive and determination. But really…if you scored a 500 on your math SAT after several tries and you don't have the study skills and ambition to improve drastically, you likely won't work for NASA as an engineer. That's why I think question 3 is important, and there's nothing wrong with that. Yes, we want to get into the career that we want. We want to be fulfilled. But we also want to set ourselves up for success. You need to look at all of your options at all times. Want to be a doctor? Have you ever heard what nurses and physician's assistants do? It's similar work, less schooling, and less bureaucracy. You may still choose to be a doctor, but you should consider all of those options.

Once you're on the right track, the work itself should be something you thrive in. If every single time you engage in that work you can't seem to complete it or see why it's necessary, this may not be the right track for you. Now, you'll hear folks in corporate and other environments tell you that the work you're doing is not going to prepare you for your career, and that may be true. But I would tell you that you need to do that work. There are transferable skills you can dig out, and the content is at least relevant. I love business and psychology. I am not a huge fan of history. If you made me study history for four years and told me that it's okay because my job would be very different from reading those books, I'd say, "Sure…but I don't enjoy the content. So… maybe I need to switch it up, yeah?"

Academics ARE important for a few reasons:

- They can be a barrier to your success if your GPA isn't high enough.
- The CONTENT will teach you a lot about your life.
- Your job may change 10,000 times over, but it's important that you use the time to build some skills.

So, what are the skills?

- Studying and research
- Focusing
- Working in groups (always try to lead your group…always
- Interacting with authority
- Following explicit directions
- Understanding that even when you follow explicit directions, you may fail to perform because the "authority" you're speaking with might be a terrible communicator
- All of the etc. (See where I'm going with this?)

And how do you build them?

- Figuring out how you work
- Setting deadlines
- Shutting down electronics to focus
- Communicating properly
- All of the etc.

I know I sound like one of your parents. Please allow me this moment. Academics do matter. I once had a student come into the final nearly an hour late. I have a rule: you can come in late, but if you come to an exam late and someone has already left (even if they finished their test in five minutes), I have no way of knowing that you didn't catch them in the parking lot, get the questions, and do a quick Google search or study before you entered my class. And I can't allow you to take the exam with your peers.

So a student entered late. Here's the conversation we had. (This has happened several times, and I am creating an amalgamation of the conversation so as to not embarrass anyone.)

- "Sorry, I can't allow you to take this exam."
- "What?? Why?"
- "Because you're over an hour late, and others have already left the exam."
- "But, you don't understand….traffic was crazy getting here!"

Now, you can insert a few other things: traffic, breakfast, I overslept, etc. Typically, students who say these things have a habit of it. They usually are late, turn in assignments late, etc. Do they all? No, I wouldn't say that, and I don't show preferential treatment to students who have better habits. Here's the bottom line: unless you were at your internship curing cancer or someone was in serious danger, I really can't show sympathy for the student who doesn't take their academics seriously. Alarms are everywhere. We have every piece of technology to help us get to where we need to go. I COMPLETELY understand that things come up. I am not a tyrant and I understand accessibility—gender-related, racial, socioeconomic, etc. I am an approachable dude in my classroom. I'll literally pick a student up for an exam. I'll pay for their bus pass or find resources for them. In order for that to happen, the student needs to take that first step and ask for help. Otherwise, I am going to view their disregard or lack of focus as privilege, and my intuition has been right plenty of times.

There are also students who really just "get it" though. One of the students who totally "got it" is a student by the name of Tanner Force. Tanner was the kind of student you dream about: intelligent, high EQ (Emotional Intelligence), driven, charismatic. Scored high on tests but was also the kind of student you could ask to present or recap something in a pinch.

- "Tanner, can you let the class know what I just said?"
- "Tanner, I am presenting to a high school tomorrow, would you be interested in being part of the Q and A?"
- "Tanner, how come I couldn't get my lesson to resonate today? What's the pulse I am missing?"

Tanner came from Southern California and took a leap to move to New York where we helped him build his career through internships in technology. If you spoke to him, you'd think him a "ditz." His classmates were always mocking his SoCal accent, blonde hair, and Abercrombie good looks (no, he was literally a model for Abercrombie). Most kids would revel in that kind of teasing, but I genuinely think he was embarrassed. Force was a humble, humble dude. If I'm honest, he was the kind of likable guy who you could look at and say "He'll do well enough with B's and a smile." He would ace any interview, lead any group, and present to anyone well.

So you'd think someone who had that many things going for him wouldn't want or need to focus on academics. But the best part about him was his humility. Force was too humble to realize he was a "cool kid." So he focused a LOT on school. And he definitely applied his humility and work ethic.

Tanner found it ironic that his classmates didn't ask how the coursework they were taking was going to benefit them:

"Once per semester, someone would take the chance to ask how the course is going to be beneficial for their career. It can be a difficult question to answer and thus equally as challenging to do well in the class. Throughout college, I saw colleagues make their academic experience miserable because they did not value the work. I felt the same way, at times. It was later into my college years that I internalized the reason that I have taken my academic education seriously."

Tanner would go on to say that the value of each class is not only from the "what" that is being learned but more from the "how" in which it is being learned.

"Approaching each assignment with this mindset motivated me to identify the hidden value in each course. One example to think of is writing a research paper. Each step in the process has an implicit learning opportunity that makes the research immensely more valuable. One of the initial steps may be taking into consideration your professor's thoughts as you choose your topic. Deciding the topic of your paper can be a dreaded task until it is perceived as an opportunity to see how stakeholder expectations impact your decisions. Trying to balance the topic selection between what interests you and what will get you a good grade is valuable implicit learning. As you complete the research paper, you may find more tasks that seem to be more trouble than good. However, these activities provide the opportunity to recognize additional skills and insights gained from the 'how' in which they are accomplished."

Academics are definitely not the ONLY thing you need to think about. I mean...if they were, I'd be writing a ten-chapter book on how to earn a 4.0. But you do need to make a connection between academics and the rest of your life. Nothing eliminates someone faster from MOST (not all) jobs than a low GPA. I also think it's cool when folks have interesting new majors:

- Data Analytics
- Sustainable Entrepreneurship
- Alternative Sports Management
- Quantitative Finance
- Etc.

There are many edges to the sword. I was in a low-GPA situation myself. I graduated from a private college with a 3.2 GPA, JUST barely high enough to be able to put it on my resume as far as my career counselors were concerned. Even then, I was a little embarrassed. And let me be clear—it's not that I was embarrassed at the number. I was embarrassed at the effort. I was in gifted classes throughout all of my formal schooling and typically opted out of the most challenging ones. In high school, I spent my time playing sports, talking to girls, and playing role-play online wrestling games (you read that correctly). In college, I ran or began around 20 different out-of-classroom organizations. To top that off:

I.
Literally.
Studied.
For.
One.
Class.

Well, make that two—Biology 1 and 2, which I consider the same heap of knowledge, just more of it.

Quant classes? Nope.
Analytics? Nope.
I barely even READ!

Finally, during my MBA, I earned a 3.8 and kind of learned how to prepare for class. That was only because I was informed that any grades lower than a B- would mean immediate removal from the program. Then, during my Ph.D., I was around a 3.8, as well (maybe a 3.9?) because of a similar rule. I wasn't able to earn anything less than a B. I remember studying during those years and actually crying. My brain and back hurt from sitting and studying....or what I thought was studying. I didn't have any skills at all.

But here's what's up...it's not the grade I think that is important. And I TRULY mean that. It's the ability to EARN that grade. And I don't mean by arguing with your professor. or worse, by asking your parents to do it. No, earning a higher than average GPA means that you have the ability to focus, be in brain pain, and win a game of the rules you hopefully clearly understand. Yes, I get it: there are other factors at play such as learning disabilities, tenured professors who don't actually care about their students' needs, etc., etc. I still maintain that if you can circumnavigate those obstacles, you can prove to an employer that you have a particular set of skills that are very much needed in the workforce: focus, tenacity, grit, and a growth mindset.

But PLEASE don't focus on that GPA too much. I once interviewed a student who was transferring to my university, trying to help them finish their coursework. They were going to get into the program. It wasn't a question of that. They had a 4.0 PERFECT GPA. After already disclosing that they had nothing to worry about, I was more concerned with their life after college. What were their:

- Hopes
- Dreams
- Interests
- Enthusiasms?

They continued to ask if their 4.0 GPA was going to transfer into our program. Unfortunately, the answer is, "No, your GPA doesn't transfer to a new university." And also, this is typically something that Admissions can answer for you. I understand the anxiety, but they had a mentor who could help find an internship or job post-graduation and they couldn't find anything exciting to bond about because they had focused so much on their GPA. This happens often. Typically, a student with a 4.0 works at a local business—grocery store, pizzeria, summer camp, etc. And they go to school and work. That's all. Hey, pay your way through school. Yes! I love it. But I would sacrifice a few tenths of a point for some extracurriculars. 1,000%. I ultimately decided to invite that student to our MBA program. I wasn't trying to sell them on something they didn't need. I honestly felt as though they could benefit from another year in school to build their skills and interests, as well as maybe take some time in an internship or something that would diversify them.

One thing we may be completely neglecting throughout this entire conversation is the learning that goes on in non-traditional institutions:

- Trade Schools
- Career Institutes
- Culinary Schools
- Military Training / Academies

Honestly…want to know the reason? Because I think those institutions actually do education way better than traditional institutions… especially traditional liberal arts institutions. There was absolutely a time in which the liberal arts schools, especially the Ivy League schools, taught folks how to think critically and network; but was that happening in school? Or was that happening in social circles? And what traditional institutions were excluding the groups we now realize have been held back for decades or centuries? Was there that much learning really going on? Or were smart, wealthy folks being taught how to find other smart, wealthy folks? Hmm….

If I could build a university today, and brand recognition was a non-issue, I'd build a competency-based school that taught skills and assessed the traits of students. It would market to the folks who showed exemplary leadership skills and critical thinking, and I'd eradicate the internet while in session. I'd allow folks to learn the way we were meant to…from one another…not flat screens and papers.

Sigh, I digress. Just stop focusing on that stupid number. Get it high enough and then build YOU.

FROM THE EXPERTS

In 2015, I finished my dissertation study, which involved something called Digital Orientation…how we adapt to technology and the way that we learn because of that adaptation. Here are some statistics from that study.

1. First of all, the study wasn't a true understanding of how we learn because I had to even the score for all three methods of learning: digital, gamified, and traditional classroom. So if the game stopped and checked in on you 30 times...so did the professor/trainer. But do professors stop 30 times to check in on you during a 20-minute lecture? They do not. So right off the bat....games and digital learning will assist those who need more check-ins, perhaps those with learning disabilities, etc. - Salute, 2015

2. There is a definite correlation between how we learn and our age. If we use some deductive logic, age is linked to digital orientation. That means the younger you are, the better you typically "speak technology." Those who "speak technology" will lean towards digital learning methods. - Salute, 2015

3. Lastly, when all things are equal (which they seldom are but had to be for the purposes of this study), all other factors are irrelevant. That means that nothing beats good old-fashioned traditional classroom learning...again...if the professor checks in as often as a digital game. Further research is needed! - Salute, 2015

PROFESSOR'S PRO TIPS

I will say this until the cows come home...if you want a strong GPA, don't focus on it. It's the same way I tell folks not to focus on money. Focus on enjoying your work and trust me...you'll make money. So focus on learning. Have you ever tried to memorize a speech or concept? What happens? You remember what you need to, vomit it out, and then it's over. You forget most of it. Now think about the times in which you tried to remember a concept and truly understand it. Perhaps you taught it to a friend or debated it over dinner with family. Did you ever forget it? No, you didn't. It's because you internalized it instead of memorizing it.

The same goes with your GPA or your work. Internalizing the work instead of memorizing the results will always yield better "stuff." Now, do you risk having a lower GPA? Sure, you do. But, will that likely happen? Eh....probably not. And let's be real—if your GPA is a 3.4 instead of a 3.8 but you actually recall the concepts you needed to, you'll land where you need to.

Another note is to pay attention to your brain. Learning disabilities are far more common than we think. And that's not a crutch. It's a thing. Our brains are DESTROYED from the internet and TV and everything else we've injected into it. So pay attention to it. If something isn't working, fix it. I hate when people say "Oh, my brain works differently so I need _____." Well, we can't teach 1,000 different ways, unfortunately. So it's on us to fix that problem first! And trust me, this is coming from someone who has fairly severe ADHD. If COVID has taught us anything, it's that there are lots of ways we can learn; but unfortunately, the one teacher in the room cannot cater to all of us. And that's not a cop-out. It's a broken system. But in the meantime, don't let that system break you, too.

Worksheet

I want you to build a document with all of the skills that you've learned in all of your classes. Then, I want you to put them all in a resume. Put the skills in the skills section. Put the "Relevant Coursework" section about your experience. And don't forget your other experience! You may use a basic version of my resume template as your base.

CHRISTOPHER SALUTE
Email / Cell
Address

PROFESSIONAL SUMMARY
Don't put an objective on your resume. Your objective is to get a job.

EDUCATION
Hofstra University, Hempstead, NY
Ph.D. in Applied Organizational Psychology, December 2015
GPA 3.8/4.0, Recruitment Committee Chair, Teacher's Assistant

Molloy College, Rockville Center, NY
M.B.A. in Management, May 2008
GPA 3.8/4.0, Sigma Beta Delta, Keynote Speaker, Leadership Scholarship

Siena College, Loudonville, NY
B.A. in Psychology, Minors in Business & Writing/Communications, May 2006
GPA: 3.2/4.0, Dean's List, National Scholars Honors Society/Dean's List,
President Scholar

OVERALL EXPERIENCE
Put your Relevant Coursework here

Classes taught in:	General Experience:
• Quantitative Analysis and Statistics • Research Methods • Marketing, fashion, sports, and management • Organizational Behavior • Business Communications and Sales • Entrepreneurship • Information Systems; Microsoft Excel	• Constantly hit sales, recruitment, and business development goals • Created print and email marketing • Created social media and SEO • Data analytics and report building • Hiring, training, and managing staff • Event planning and execution

SELECT RELEVANT EXPERIENCE

- Company, Address, Years
- Blah
  ◦ Blah
  ◦ Blah

COMPUTER SKILLS

You can make this a "Skills and Languages" Section for now

All Social Media and Blogging Sites, Graphic Design, Mail Order Manager, Yahoo! Stores, Intactix, Mas90, Mas500, Amazon.com, Approach, Vendornet, Buy.com, Sears Marketplace, Siebel, IBIS, Mortgage Cadence, Genesis, Coyote, Traks, Quark, Adobe Premiere, Adobe Photoshop, Adobe Illustrator, Enco, Visual Basics, C++, PowerPoint, Microsoft Office, VoxPro, Pro Tools, Internet Audio Vault, Powergold, Cool Edit Pro, eBay, Turbo Lister, Vendio, Goldmine, UPS, Basic HTML, Certified in Microsoft Excel, Powerpoint, Word

NAME

Email / Cell

Address

PROFESSIONAL SUMMARY

EDUCATION

OVERALL EXPERIENCE

SELECT RELEVANT EXPERIENCE

SKILLS & LANGUAGES

_____
_____
_____
_____

CHAPTER 8
OUTSIDE OF THE CLASSROOM

On March 12th, 2019…just as the COVID pandemic was REALLY beginning…we absolutely didn't need a reason to focus on this story. But we had all of the time in the world. Good thing, because we were really interested in the 50 people (including Lori Laughlin, famous star of the TV show *Full House*) who were sentenced after a trial that involved the "fixing" or "rigging" of standardized testing.

From NBC News:

"Authorities said the FBI investigation, code-named Operation Varsity Blues, uncovered a network of wealthy parents who paid thousands of dollars to a California man who boosted their children's chances of gaining entrance into elite colleges, such as Yale and Stanford, by paying people to take tests for their children, bribing test administrators to allow that to happen, and bribing college coaches to identify the applicants as athletes." https://www.nbcnews.com/news/us-news/feds-uncover-massive-college-entrance-exam-cheating-plot-n982136

This is a problem. It's a major one. But the problem isn't that these parents did what they did. And it's not that students went along with it. The problem is with the system itself.

I have a mentor who loves to talk about and quote Malcolm Gladwell. Have you read Malcolm Gladwell? Books like *Outliers*, for example? They both (my mentor and Dr. Gladwell) say to picture your intelligence like height on a basketball court. If you're 5'4", can you play in the NBA? Not likely, no matter how good you are—the very rare Muggsy Bogues or Spud Webb. Isaiah Thomas was 5'9". But these folks are not the norm.

Now, can you play in the NBA if you're 6'8"? Yes, you can actually! But you also need to be a skilled player. Right? Dribbling, passing, scoring, footwork, etc.

Now....answer me this...is there a major difference between someone who is 6'8" and someone who is 6'11" in the NBA? How about a human being who is 9 feet tall? Would they be at an advantage?

The answer...probably not. Once you're tall enough to stand amongst the titans in that league, all of the other stuff matters more: dribbling, passing, scoring....LEADERSHIP. Right?

The same goes for your intelligence...which is measured by these ridiculous standardized tests. There's a reason that a lot of CEOs are not 1600 SAT-ers. There's also a reason that many of them drop out of school. Once you're smart ENOUGH, you need to really focus on other parts of yourself: leadership, charisma, presentation skills, delegation, your ability to connect with folks, focus, the arts, and being cultured...right?

Imagine this: you're about to go on a date with someone who, on paper, has everything you want. They are attractive, have a great job, the same values as you, etc. You get to the date. You sit down to dinner. They say nothing. You try to make conversation. They give you one-word answers. They grunt and nod. They didn't shower so they have a bit of an aroma that interrupts your senses while you eat. Are you going on a second date?

Life is all about that connection. Someone can look great on paper, but it doesn't make them right for you...for the job you're looking to hire for...for the gig you have...as your partner...whatever!

Dating aside, let's talk about an actual applicable scenario. Have you ever heard of the "lunch test?" Likely not because it's something my colleagues and I use. Let's describe it:

Do you know why I usually conduct my interviews before lunch? Because I cannot focus on anything but menial tasks after lunch. follow-ups, data, emails, etc. I try to get all of my meetings done when I have the most energy. Makes sense, right? This is something a lot of folks do. It also means you can loosen your tie and/or worry a bit less about meeting new people. Nobody likes to worry about all that stuff all day.

So picture this...you're at an interview. It's 11:00 a.m. and I (or your interviewer) has lunch at 12:00 noon. When I was in sales, the team used to always take lunch around the same time. It built camaraderie, gave us all a break in the day, etc. Not to mention, nobody is at their desks during lunch so we can't call folks. We used to go to lunch at one of two cafes nearby; let me tell you...the food was incredible. One of them was a test kitchen for a really well-known restaurant chain. The other was a cafe attached to a retail shop. There was a guy on our team...literally one of the best reps in the organization. Might have actually been the wealthiest guy on the floor...including some of the managers. And he'd be eyeing your dish before you put your fork down.

"Hey...you think you're gonna eat that garlic bread?"

"Uh...yeah, bro...I do think I'm going to eat my garlic bread...relax about it." That garlic bread was amazing.

Anyway, I'm interviewing you at 11:00 for a role in our organization. And I'm thinking about my garlic bread. You've got to keep up with my questions and keep my attention, right? We have a few back and forths. I ask you questions. You answer with some great stories about why you're awesome. You ask me some questions that show me you're engaged in what I have to say. Maybe you even throw in a few zingers about how you've looked into my background on LinkedIn or ask me what I love most about working there. Impressive!

Now, here's where the lunch test comes in. We're going to chat about the job, we're going to chat about you, and myself, and all of the things that pertain to work. What we're not going to do is get personal because that's inappropriate. But what is appropriate is me picturing if you're going to fit in with our team. Remember that you spend more time with work than you spend with almost anyone else in your life. If you count sleep, your spouse or partner edges everyone else out.

So, all the while, I'm picturing whether or not you're going to get along with folks. Will you complain when there's a team project? Not want to work with so and so? Will you be pleasant? Kind? Maybe funny? Or do you have a negative attitude that will spread through my organization until you ultimately leave?

When I first started my career, I had a few managers who would ask our teams to stay late. My favorite was my mentor and manager, Jacqueline. She'd come into the office after an entire day of collecting training ideas from our sales team (we ran the corporate training team). Some were due the next day…yes, I understand this is crazy. But at around 3:00 p.m. she'd come into my office and say "Hey, want White Castle tonight?" That was code for "We'll be here past dinner time." Totally cool with me because I love White Castle, I love hanging with Jacqueline, and I love being a valued member of the team. So it was my pleasure to do so. If that weren't an atmosphere I thrived in, I wouldn't have fit in that organization. And it's likely that would have been evident in the interview after chatting with folks about who I am, what my values are, etc.

So, back to you—you're interviewing with me. And I am about to head to lunch. I am thinking about whether or not you're going to fit into the organization. I am hoping you will, of course! Your goal is for me to think about inviting you to lunch for that reason, to get to know each other more and to see if you really can hang with the team. Or perhaps you've already made a great impression, and I am excited to meet a more "casual you." If I don't want to invite you to lunch, it's likely that I've already come to the conclusion that you're not the right fit.

Now, I want to be clear….I am NOT inviting you to lunch. That's inappropriate. The point is that I should be curious about you. That's the point of the "lunch test." Being able to do the job should be fairly evident in your resume. And, honestly, even then I'd want to see you on the job, right? There are other great things we can do to figure out your qualifications:

- References
- An in-basket test (we give you some tasks to do)
- A shadow day
- Personality trait tests (these do get a little hairy because of various biases)

So, this really is about fit. Are you an interesting candidate?

Now, it is 2021 so I want to address where the lunch test can go wrong. Fit is subjective. Fit is tough to gauge. Fit can ALSO be:

- Racist
- Sexist
- Ageist
- Discriminant against weight
- Discriminant against looks
- Discriminant against sexual orientation
- Subject to so many awful things

This is why your HR Director or interviewers HAVE GOT TO BE on point with their integrity. If they are not, we're all in big trouble. Now there is something called a "BFOQ" which is a Bona Fide Occupational Qualification. THAT makes it okay to actually look at race, sex/gender, etc. For example, if you're looking for a historically black figure for a play…you can only look at black men for that role. When I hired writers for a plus-size media publication, I looked to hire plus-sized women because they experienced what they were writing about …versus me…who didn't.

But when does that become an issue? Let's discuss a situation that I actually experienced…

When I was consulting for a web company in my mid-twenties, I came across a mid-sized firm that was big in e-commerce. By mid-sized I mean revenue-wise. Actual staff? Very small. I was in charge of hiring, training, and managing the customer service, sales, and operations teams. Honestly, I did everything but accounting. So when I was interviewing to staff up the customer service team, the owner of the company suggested that I put a photo of his kids at my desk...

"Put this photo on your desk. You can't ask if women have children... but you can have that start a conversation about whether or not they have kids and if their parenting or family needs will get in the way of work."

I was appalled. I was actually in shock. I was young and wanted to keep my job so I didn't say anything at the time. He did ask me if I'd used his photo after interviews and I just said "No, I didn't." I didn't say that I forgot or that I would next time. But I also didn't say that I was opposed to it, as I should have. But that was the beginning of the end for us.

There were other inconsistencies about his policy on health insurance, general hygiene in the office and warehouse that I couldn't live with, as well. But it was all indicative of someone with low integrity. So it was for the best that I made moves to leave that organization.

"The Lunch Test" really is more about demeanor and interest. What are you all about? Were you an athlete? Thespian? Mathlete? Student Government member? That's what I want to know...outside of the resume, are you human?

So, how do you become human? Hopefully, you already are! But you know what I mean. One thing that really kills me is when I ask young folks what they do after class and they say "nothing" or "play video games/hang out with friends." Look, I am not saying we all need to be the captain of the debate team, but there has to be something that interests them after school! Nowadays, there are so many incredible options for students. There's probably an e-sports club you can join or start! After-school jobs and internships? Do SOMETHING...please...not for me...for you. Not just because it's important that you get into the career of your dreams, but because life is so much more fulfilling when you do things that stimulate you. I can say this with CERTAINTY: when I pick up my phone and "hang out" or "play around" for hours, I feel my body get exhausted and my brain is so weak. Yes, sometimes relaxing is good. But when I pick up a pen and write or do something crafty or fight Mixed Martial Arts, I feel 1000x better.

Nobody is asking you to do anything entirely out of your comfort zone. But…a little bit? Yes. When I was in middle school, I wanted to quit the lacrosse team (I was absolutely awful). My father told me I had to do something after school, and I burst into tears. I wasn't really good at anything. I loved singing and acting, but I never learned to read sheet music in elementary school and I was afraid to ask for help. I just quit things instead of admitting I didn't know something. ALSO, a bad move.

Then, there was college me. Ready? I was told by my freshman year that I could be like my student idol. His resume was framed in the career services office, and I wanted mine to be just like this: student government, radio station, TV station, etc. It was awesome!

So what did I do? By the end of my senior year, I'd founded or was the president of nearly 20 organizations on campus, from our radio station and TV station to our literary journal and comic book club. But I took on too much. I wound up being asked to step down from some positions because I just didn't have the time to do it all. Heck, I still get myself into those situations. Hmm…maybe I need to stop those patterns. Next book!

You need to find a happy mid-point. Don't take on too much, but DO NOT BE A GPA or test score. Look…let's be frank for a second. Our educational system is in major disarray. It needs serious reform. So priding yourself on a global stage for your grades…meh…that's a game you likely won't win. There are folks in other countries who have more knowledge than you and have been trained by a better education system, etc. All that jazz. So what can you bring to the table that is not plain old intelligence?

I've gone on for nearly five pages…all to tell you…what?

You need to diversify your interests. And that doesn't just include clubs and committees. Yes, you should absolutely be involved with teams and such…and I don't care if you're an introvert…be uncomfortable for a bit because you're going to be throughout your life. But you also want to think about:

- Culture
- Finance
- Sports
- Arts
- Music
- Books
- Entertainment
- Crypto
- Entrepreneurship
- Outdoors
- Etc.

You're going to be in situations where you need to show someone two things:

- Your ability to work in a structured setting
- Your ability to be entrepreneurial

I mean, shoot, you may even BE an entrepreneur at some point. At that point, is anyone going to care what your GPA was? Does a bank need to know how well you did in chemistry when giving you a land loan for your building? Spoiler Alert…NOPE!

And don't tell me you're not interested in anything. EVERYONE is. I have to say…I caught that movie *Soul* recently…the Disney one. WHAT A MOVIE. It was just something we threw on for background noise, and I had to rewatch it because it was INCREDIBLE. What's the key point: everyone has something they are in love with. Find that and you'll be fine. I am not going to tell you the whole "never work a day in your life" thing. Because that's trash garbage.

Work.
Work hard.
Do things that make you uncomfortable.
Learn and grow.
Never stop.
And you'll be fine.

You have to learn WHO YOU ARE before you know WHERE YOU FIT.

PROFESSOR'S PRO TIPS

This chapter is all about finding yourself outside of the classroom. Look, I know the "lunch test" seems old school and potentially problematic. As a 2021 New Age mentor, I get that. But it doesn't change the fact that you need to be aware that folks are going to perceive you a certain way. So show your best self and be interesting. But also show your genuine self.

Remember: the best opportunities are the ones that fit YOU. Seriously, be yourself and if you miss out on something…it's probably because a judgmental cheeseball doesn't like your hair color or something. Sure, you can probably make a case out of that. But would you want to work there?

I remember when I interviewed with that person I mentioned above (who used the children's photo). I had maybe 40 minutes prior to my interview. So I was in a coffee shop bathroom looking at my suit, my hair…my earrings…I called my partner and asked her, "Hey, should I take these earrings out?"

> "What do you think? Will it impact your interview?" She was being genuine.
>
> "I may not get it with these in."

I took them out and forgot to put them back in ever again. Months later I asked my CEO if he would have hired me with earrings in.

"You were already the youngest candidate. That would have been a definite no from me."

Did I learn a lot? Yes. But that organization was not the right fit for me. Maybe I should have kept the earrings in. See what I mean?

FROM THE EXPERTS

1. Nationally, 83 percent of all children ages 6 to 17 participated in at least one extracurricular activity, including clubs, sports, or lessons. - www.urban.org

2. Children tend to have higher levels of school engagement when involved in one or more activities, like sports, lessons, or clubs. - US Census Bureau, 2018

3. Several studies, including a recent one from Texas A&M, correlate extracurricular activities with better learning outcomes (and often GPA, although not directly quoted in this study) - www.nordangliaeducation.com

WORKSHEET

Believe it or not...an obscene amount of college students still swear by a paper calendar and planner. So I am not going to give you a spreadsheet to track your extracurriculars...even though I REALLY want to.

Instead, I am going to give you this very simple skills checklist that I have developed. I would suggest picking three skills you want to learn outside of the classroom. If you're an introvert, at least one needs to be through a club or organization. If you're an extrovert, one needs to be done alone.

List your milestones. For example, I wanted to learn Spanish a few years back. So one milestone may have been to have a conversation with someone who also speaks Spanish. Set your milestones and knock them off when you've completed them.

SKILL:

How are you achieving this?
_____
_____

Is this an organized or solo activity?
_____

Beginning Date:
_____

Milestone 1: _____
Milestone 1 Date Achieved:
_____

Milestone 2: _____
Milestone 2 Date Achieved:
_____

Milestone 3: _____
Milestone 3 Date Achieved:
_____

Milestone 4: _____
Milestone 4 Date Achieved:
_____

Milestone 5: _____
Milestone 5 Date Achieved:
_____

CHAPTER 9
PRESENTATIONS AND PAPERS

When I was an upper-class person in my undergraduate degree program, I decided to add a Minor in Business to my quite useless Bachelor's Degree in Psychology. This forced me to take some fairly low-level classes in business at an older age. It was fun: new people to argue with, new things to learn, and probably some easy A's to boost my C's in biology and quantitative analysis (yes, I did poorly in technical classes until I embraced my nerd-dom during my MBA and PhD studies).

It also meant being paired with folks I didn't know during group projects. In the Psych department, you knew everyone. You began taking classes with the same folks over and over. You knew who was going to sit where, who was going to speak up (or in my case, be obnoxious). You knew who your best lab partners were. You had your friends, etc.

But in business classes, I knew nobody, which meant when it was time to pair up for group assignments, I was the loser who waited around looking for someone to pick me. Luckily, marketing class came naturally to me. I had fairly intelligent things to say, and my natural leadership ability kind of took over where my content knowledge didn't. So when it was time to select groups for our marketing project, a few underclass-folks approached me during class and asked if I would join them. Desperate and scared that nobody liked me, of course, I said yes.

I'm going to be super honest. I don't remember most of putting the project together with them. I remember we divided the work evenly. It was a small project, so we only had a few weeks. Most of us lived on campus, so we met in the dorms. I remember going to their dorm because I was the only one who lived in an upper-class building (buildings were typically divided by class year, with some exceptions). And we put together a pretty awesome PowerPoint presentation. Well…pretty awesome for a few hours of work…let's be real.

We went over the presentation a few times, divided it up based on our strong suits, and prepped for presentation day. Normal stuff. What I wasn't aware of was the fact that a lot of these younger students had not really presented much before. Perhaps they were afraid to say? Perhaps they thought I hadn't either? Maybe they didn't think it was relevant to mention? Who knows, right?

So on the day of the presentation, I put on a button-up and tie, fixed my hair, sprayed on some of my fancy good cologne (not the everyday spray!), and took the trek up to the north side of campus. (This is a joke to anyone who knows how small a campus Siena College is.) Our presentation team was confident. So we decided to go early on during the class. Not first, but definitely the second.

The presentation began fairly well. It was running smoothly… normally. We'd rehearsed who would go when. I led off and passed it on to one of my colleagues. They stumbled a bit through their presentation. Passed it off a little early. Okay, we got this. Partner three spoke for all of 18 seconds…and concluded. Oh, dear. Partner 4? Blank. Partner 5? Cold sweats. We had about 4 minutes of a 15-minute presentation done. What in the hell?

The presentation was on a consumer good. I had no stinking clue what to do. But I did remember a few things:

- I'd presented before
- I was also a theater nerd as a kid
- Nobody knows what is going on but you and your team

So I did the first thing that came to mind: I channeled Chris Farley in *Tommy Boy*. Okay, okay…just wait for it. I wasn't as over the top! But there are a few scenes where he just goes a little off the reservation and delivers some "what if" scenarios to potential clients.

> *Tommy*: Let's think about this for a sec, Ted. Why do they put a guarantee on a box? Hmm, very interesting.
> *Ted*: I'm listening.
> *Tommy*: Here's how I see it. A guy puts a guarantee on the box 'cause he wants you to feel all warm and toasty inside.
> *Ted*: Yeah, makes a man feel good.
> *Tommy*: 'Course it does. Ya think if you leave that box under your pillow at night, the Guarantee Fairy might come by and leave a quarter.
> *Ted*: What's your point?
> *Tommy*: The point is, how do you know the Guarantee Fairy isn't a crazy glue sniffer? "Building model airplanes," says the little fairy, but we're not buying it. Next thing you know, there's money missing off the dresser, and your daughter's knocked up. I seen it a hundred times.
> *Ted*: But why do they put a guarantee on the box then?
> *Tommy*: Because they know all they sold ya was a guaranteed piece of shit. That's all it is. Hey, if you want me to take a dump in a box and mark it guaranteed, I will. I got spare time. But for right now, for your sake, for your daughter's sake, ya might wanna think about buying a quality item from me.
> *Ted*: Hmm. Okay, I'll buy from you.
> *Tommy*: Well I… What?

Tommy Boy didn't care if he sounded a little crazy…because he was getting the job done. So, I did the same.

"So, I know what you're all thinking!" I proclaimed as I found the nearest empty chair. I turned, kicked off, and landed in it, sliding to the back of the room. "Why would I buy this? TOTALLY valid reasoning. We haven't sold you yet." I popped out of the chair and began to run through:

- Marketing
- Financials
- Projections

As I went through each section of the presentation we'd gone through together, I called on my teammates to answer questions, which they did happily. I then concluded, we got a huge applause from our classmates, and the professor asked some questions. She seemed impressed with us, or at least me. But the feedback she gave in our grade was that our presentation was too "me" heavy. We got an A- overall because our paper was an A paper and our presentation was a B due to lack of equal participation. Do I let her know that my team froze up? That I was just doing what I felt was necessary to finish the presentation?

The answer: No. Don't throw your team under the bus, whether you've known each other for a decade or a minute. That's the wrong way to create loyalty and positivity. The bottom line was that we could have prepared more together. We could have gone through the presentation over and over in front of friends, ourselves, etc. I should have recognized their level of inexperience and realized that they could use more practice. So I took the grade that was given, and we didn't speak a word of it. After class, they did come up to me privately and thank me for that herculean effort.

What are some takeaways from this stupid and silly story? Presentations require preparation. As do papers. But we often get into this ridiculous pattern of:

- Cram
- Regurgitate
- Cram
- Regurgitate
- Cram
- Reg....you get the point.

This works for a standardized test. It may even work for a one-time paper or quick presentation. But people who know what they are looking for will see right through you and all of that. So, what do you do?

Memorize?
Nope.

Internalize.
Yes. That's the ticket!

Now, let's be clear: a little dramatic effect can't hurt. But VERY little. I had a student who would wait for dead silence, and he had these amazing wooden soles on his shoes. He'd wait for that silence in the room, no matter how long it took, then pace from the back of the classroom to the front and begin speaking…

"What if you could change the world with the touch of an app?" he'd ask. I mean, you could say that about almost any app, can't you? But the way he said it was stupendous! I took him and a group of his peers to a business public speaking competition one year…our absolute first year in the competition…and we swept it. 12 Students, 12 trophies. I'd be lying if I said I didn't borrow great tips from some of them to give to the other students. They had some fire!

My one-off "Chris Farley" drama was not something I got used to when I presented. Most of my presentations were straightforward, analytic, and organized. I was usually persuasive, but that's about it. I grew up enjoying music and drama, but I didn't think either of them had any place in the boardroom. I was smart enough to carry a room on my own without that. And God, I hated when someone had their presentation mapped out like a damn infomercial. "Okay, now take it away with those financials…Amber!" Shut up!

That was until I met Charles Garcia. I interviewed Chuck for a position at my university about a year into my position as Assistant Dean. I was arrogant, just a bit younger, and very insecure. I was asked to interview an ex-finance professional who had a binder full of pedagogy and teaching principles. The only problem was he'd never taught! So, since I had no idea who he was and I was an arrogant, obnoxious human, I wasn't as engaged as I should have been during the first few minutes of our conversation. That was until he dropped the three last (and I think only) organizations he'd worked at. They were all Fortune 100, enormous, and very well-respected. I leaned in.

And that was the beginning and the end of my arrogance around... well, anyone. It was also the beginning of a wonderful relationship. I thought I was done learning when I met him. It was through him and a few others that I realized what makes a great professor is the ability to never stop learning. So what did I learn?

Garcia was a master presenter. He had the ability to engage a room of anyone, anywhere, and used any means necessary. Jumping on desks, throwing things (safely), shouting, etc. But it was while learning his style that I realized that one can be professional and entertaining and that the two were not mutually exclusive. Whether it was stopping someone mid-presentation to put on his "dad tone" and correct them, letting them know they could do better, or surprising everyone with a new quote and exhibition of that quote, he was always leveling up.

What was his biggest level up? It was the building of confidence. And that is the key to both presentations and papers—confidence. Confidence does not mean knowing everything...because that's impossible...and that's also arrogance. Confidence is knowing what it feels like to fail yet still proceed even though you may not have every answer. But you're okay finding them all out.

Garcia not only has this confidence but makes it his mission to instill it in his students. He does this through climbing and hiking. You see, when you bring 30 or so students to one of the tallest peaks in the Northeast and get every single student to summit (summit means top) with little to no preparation, you show them one thing...that they can do anything if they stop pretending to be perfect and fail in front of each other. This is a lesson he teaches over and over but the first time you witness it, it is truly awesome. Picture it: 20-30 students, mostly from cities and suburbs, many of whom have never traveled outside of the metro area or hiked anywhere, driving up to Mount Marcy for a weekend getaway. Many of them are not acquainted yet. It's a highly competitive program, and they don't know who their friends are or who will be. With instructions from Chuck Garcia, they wake up super early on a Saturday morning. They are driven to the bottom of a mountain. They spend the rest of the morning and afternoon hiking up and down a seriously rigorous trail and the evening eating take-out food and s'mores. The next day, we'd drive home bonded but the students also had a sense of accomplishment that was unrivaled by most other activities. The trip showed them that it was okay to fail, but it was way more fun to be successful. And once you've figured out that you can fail, you do it much less often. You will take calculated risks and be much more genuine in all things. And you'll welcome challenges and feedback because they will make you better!

Presentations are not just about controlling the room but controlling your emotions. The same can be said about academic papers, which Garcia usually hates. I am not that fond of most of them, either, mostly because they are drab and lack energy. Few students go into a presentation with the want to learn. They just want to be done. The same can be said of papers. Students aren't trying to learn but to prove that they know enough about a topic to have a coherent conversation. And do you ever really know enough?

So I've given you a brief understanding of what I hate about most college papers. I don't want to harp on that. Let's instead talk about how to write a great paper and how it SHOULD be completed.

First, let's get this part over with. Your professor doesn't hate you and actually does want you to learn through the writing of this paper. MOST of them will read the entire thing. (I am sorry to say that I have had some professors who clearly had not read my papers: no feedback at all, blatant mistakes they didn't catch, etc). But you should feel confident that your paper will be read. If it isn't, send me your paper and I'll read it.

Now, I am about to say a few things you are not going to like. Are you ready? Here we go:

1. You should not be reading and researching as you write your paper. There's a great line in the movie *With Honors*...have you seen it? Joe Pesci? Brendan Frasier? Who am I kidding? I just lost all my credibility with you by naming a movie from the 1990s. Anyway, there's a line that Pesci says to Frasier, "I am doing like you, 'Harvard'...read first and then write." What

does that mean? It means that you want to make yourself a pseudo-expert on a topic before you write. Why? Because you are missing stuff in your paper that you don't know because you haven't read it yet! Also…dude…have you ever had to rewrite a paper because you accidentally deleted it? How fast did you write that thing? And how much better was it the second time? This isn't a fluke. This is the real deal. Your work will flow way better because you know where you're heading. Trust me.

2. Outline. Dude…OUT…LINE. You'll be so organized when you do that. And you'll be amazed at how easy it'll be and how well it will read. Your intro, your conclusion, it'll all flow and be so attractive. Your professor will be pleased.

3. Keep collecting sources. You're better off having more than less…this goes back to the first bullet. And find something better than a website. Go go to the library. Do the work. You'll LOVE what you learn. This sounds like a contradiction to #1, but it's not. Because by the time you've started to write, you're a pseudo-expert. You know a good portion of what you need to know. It doesn't mean you know everything. You can trust that if you continue to search for sources, you're not going to find anything groundbreaking that will make you rewrite your paper. That is…of course…IF you have done #1 properly.

4. Speaking of your professor, go see them during the process. Ask questions, show them a draft. Imagine a professor giving you a C on a paper they helped you write…their own EGO won't let that happen! Kidding…sort of. But even if your paper isn't amazing by the end of the process, just having their help is going to make it better…or at least more to their liking.

5. Auto Spell check. The end…it takes two seconds.

6. Read it over yourself, as well…OUT LOUD. You'll catch weird awkward sentences and grammar issues.

7. If you can, ask your roommate or friend to read it. Do the same for them. They will make it better.

8. Lastly, if your professor uses a rubric, ask to see it so that you can grade your own paper. Ask humbly…because they may get defensive. They may see it as you challenging their grading, which you're not. You're trying to fit your paper to their assignment.

So, you're about to tell me a bunch of things like…the fact that you don't plan ahead like this…you don't have this kind of time…and your professor is an arrogant jerk. Okay, let's break a few of these items down for you. Do you like my bullet points? I figure it'll be easier for you to follow since this topic isn't the most exciting. Check it:

- Why don't you plan ahead like this? How are your grades? Are they straight As? Do you want them to be? Do you HATE writing papers last minute and being stressed for weeks, working your ass off for an entire day only to receive a B? Right…so…do the stuff.

- I promise you that this isn't going to waste your time. This is going to SAVE YOU TIME because being an expert means fewer rewrites, fewer stops, and you'll likely be done WAY early. How many times have you asked to do extra credit because your paper didn't get you the grade you wanted? This will get you the grade, and it will save you time.

- Your professor could very well be an arrogant jerk…I've met many. But they can also just be stressed or have a fraud complex and feel like they don't know your topic well enough. We are human too, you know! Talk to your professor like a human being. Tell them how important learning this topic is to you and that you want to do it right. If they still respond negatively, you've done the best you can, and at least they know YOU are human.

Now…you're reading all of this and you're thinking "How does this dude know any of this, and why should I take him seriously?" Well…I…am…so…glad… you asked. Check this out…

I remember, vividly, hating to write papers growing up. So many teachers left me feedback like "Is this complete?" or "Would you like to rewrite this and return it to me?" And as I graduated to each grade or school level and finally learned everything I was supposed to learn, my arrogance blinded me and I went back to old habits! Still writing incompletely or switching tone/style or being lazy as heck! Who does that?

My feedback switched from "Do you want to rewrite this?" to "How have you gotten this far? This writing is terrible." I was asked to write a research paper, and I got too creative. I was asked to write a creative writing piece, and I didn't look at it from the right angle. I was asked to write a position piece, and I didn't take a position! Even colleagues I was writing group papers with called my writing "too fluffy" or "scattered" because I was trying to change the assignment.

But, I will say this: every time I had to learn a new style of writing (or re-learn because I was lazy as heck), the responses from my professors were glowing. I remember one specific professor gave me an A in the entire course because my final paper was one of the best he'd seen. This was after he called me one of the worst writers he'd ever met. Now, of course, he took credit for all of my success in writing that paper, which I absolutely did not argue with. And we wound up becoming colleagues and friends later.

With all of that back and forth, up and down…it wasn't until I consistently wrote that I realized where my flaws were. It wasn't until I earned my Ph.D. and wrote my dissertation that I truly understood what "read then write" actually meant. I didn't understand check-ins, rubrics, or actually writing with the intent to learn and educate. I sent it to everyone I could to get feedback, even if they had no idea what the content was. (Who would? "Digital Orientation and the Efficacy of

Game-Based Training Platforms on Engagement and Knowledge Retention" even bores me). I focused, refocused, and became an expert in the few niche areas I needed to. When I defended it, I certainly had some learning to do. But I was confident in what I had written.

Do you need to complete a 200+ page dissertation to learn how to write? No! In fact, don't do that. Do not be like me. Learn early. Make mistakes early. Write consistently. Follow the eight points I have outlined above and be humble. When someone says you haven't written an A paper…you haven't. Do you know why? Because you don't get to assign yourself a grade. So, play by the rules…and you may even learn a few things while you're at it.

PROFESSOR'S PRO TIP

I really had to narrow down the stories I wanted to tell about presentations, reading, researching, and learning. But in all of the stories, in all of the students I have taught and learned from, in all of the mentors I have had, there is one thing that is glaringly obvious: the way you communicate is the way you are perceived. Sounds stupid, doesn't it? Of course, you'd be perceived the way you communicate. But not everyone understands that. Not everyone realizes that their brain isn't mapped out in front of who they are talking to. They get frustrated, argumentative even.

I remember a student who was trying to enter my university. We had scheduled an interview and focused on their desire to be an entrepreneur. I said, "Tell me more about your business idea." To which they replied, "Okay…it's called 'Opulence'…everything will be luxurious and grand."

"Okay, awesome," I said… "Tell me more."

They were dumbfounded. They basically repeated the same thing. What was it? A car company? A restaurant? A clothing line? What the heck were they actually talking about?

This is not an independent event. It happens to me all the time. I am speaking with someone, young or old, colleague, friend, student, etc. And I can't understand what they are saying because they have not given themselves the opportunity to communicate properly. They think that their brain is visible to me. They get frustrated. They even get angry when I can't see what they are saying.

As an educator, if someone cannot understand what I am saying, I take complete ownership. In fact, I take it as far as "If several of my students don't pass my test, I didn't communicate properly." It's always going to be my fault first.

You can absolutely be one of the smartest people in the room...but if you cannot articulate your thoughts, you are lost. Someone with half of your intelligence and drive will beat you to the punch every time. I've heard this from mentor after mentor: Speak swiftly, but well. You don't have to be the smartest. You don't even have to have the best idea. What you have to do is communicate your idea first and well.

FROM THE EXPERTS

1. A tweet posted by a 15-year-old high-school student said to "Stop forcing students to present in front of the class and give them a choice not to." This tweet garnered more than 130,000 re-tweets and nearly half a million likes. This is a mistake, and it is destroying the way young folks are communicating. Exposure therapy is real and it combats anxiety beautifully. - *The Atlantic*

2. According to CivicScience.com, those who had a 2.5 GPA or lower in college are, in fact, the most likely to make under $25k, and under $50k. BUT...check this out... 21% of that same group makes more than $150k each year, which is the largest percentage of any GPA in the U.S. college population

3. In that same study, the differences in salary percentages between those with a 3.1-3.5 GPA and those with a 3.5-4.0 GPA looked NEARLY identical.

What do the last few statistics tell you? That GPA is not as valuable as you might think. So, focus on other factors that will get you the job and will keep you there.

Worksheet

This worksheet can be used for either a presentation or a paper. In either circumstance, practice makes perfect. Yeah, yeah…stop rolling your eyes.

Beginning with the due date, work backward until you can establish a timeline for your project.

Due Date: _____

Submission: _____
(Should be at least 1 day prior…technology can kill you)

Final Submission Completed
by:_____
(Should be 1 day prior so you can read it once more and correct anything)

Retrieve Draft back from colleague:
_____
(Should be 2 days prior to submission)

Draft sent to friend or colleague: _____
(Should be 4 days prior to the submission date so that they can give you input.
And sent to someone new. DO NOT WAIT THIS LONG TO SEND IT TO A PROFESSOR. You should know what they want by now.)

Final Draft (not final paper Complete): _____
(1 day prior to sending it to a friend or colleague. 5 Days before Submission. 6 days before due date)

Second Draft Review: _____
(10 days prior to Final Draft Completion)

Retrieve Draft back from colleague: _____
(Should be 12 days prior to Final Draft Completion)

Second Draft sent to friend/colleague or professor):
_____ (Should be 16 days prior to Final Draft Completion and sent to someone new)

Second Draft Complete: _____
(Should be 18 days prior to Final Draft Completion)

First Draft Review by yourself:_____
(20 days prior to Final Draft Completion)

Retrieve First Draft back from review: _____
(Should be 22 days prior to Final Draft Completion)

First Draft sent to friend/colleague or professor:
_____ (Should be 26 days prior to Final Draft Completion)

First Draft Complete: _____
(Should be 28 days prior to Final Draft Completion)

Outline Completed:_____
(Should be 10 days prior to First Draft Completion)

Research Completed: _____ (Should be 2 days before Outline Completion)

Research Begun:_____
(Should be 10 days prior to Outline Completion)

Review Rubric: _____
(Should be as soon as you receive your assignment)

Now, obviously, if your paper or presentation is due sooner, you can alter these timelines. This is built for a large, senior-level paper!

CHAPTER 10
THE INTERVIEW

"I am so scared," said one of my colleagues. "This is the first time I am interviewing anyone."

There you have it. Even your interviewer is scared. They don't know what to do. They don't know what to say. They don't know who you are. So, relax! But you're going to relax ONLY because you've prepared so well, right? Let's talk about that.

I had a student at my university once, Ryan Caldwell, who more than a few folks said I needed to meet. I couldn't figure out why. I was running a department of highly trained and very detail-oriented advisors. Our job was to make sure students were registered, comfortable, and on a track to graduation and a successful career. So, with a caseload of 80 to 120 students each, why were so many folks telling me about one student?

Ryan was out of place. He had left a much larger university system to come to our smaller school. There are considerably fewer opportunities to network with alumni, have a typical campus life, etc. But, we excelled in something his much larger school didn't: customization. A kid like Ryan needed way more networking than any college experience would have given him, even his larger school. But at a school like ours, he wouldn't have found a vast network unless someone discovered him. His ambition way outweighed that of his peers. He was a competitive swimmer, sailor, and if I remember correctly, worked at a golf course over the summers. Or did he belong to one? I don't recall. But Caldwell was used to chatting it up with Long Island North Shore powerhouses. He wasn't going to be happy at a career fair with small insurance companies or joining the astronomy club.

When I met him, towering over 6 feet tall, perfectly pristine haircut, and pressed clothes, I got it. This kid lived differently. He wasn't rolling into my office in pajamas. He was nervous, the kind of nervous you'd get before a big game. You can win it, but there's someone on the other side of the court against you...i.e. me. I assured Ryan that we were just a couple of kids having a chat and asked him why so many folks had recommended I meet with him.

"I just don't know where to go from here," said Ryan. Ryan knew that he would get bored easily or fall into partying, etc. We discussed his past, but that was what was least important to me. I was more interested in what he wanted to do with his future. Ryan had no idea, but he had been meeting with some alumni in finance, which was a good start.

Ryan could likely sell anything. He just had a charisma about him that was irresistible. When folks don't know what they want to do, they tend to end up in sales. So some of the folks he'd already been meeting with were in financial sales.

Why financial sales? Because Ryan was also a strategist. He understood the push and pull of relationships. I had a mentor who told me once:

"Look, if you're good with people...you can sell. And you can spend your time selling a can of Pepsi over and over and over. Figure a can of Pepsi costs 10 cents wholesale. What's your commission on that? Now how about Pepsi stock? How much does that cost, and how much is your commission? How many cans of Pepsi will you have to sell to make up the commission on 1,000 shares of Pepsi?"

So I followed this logic for any of my charismatic, intelligent, strategy-driven students. Ryan was no exception. But...like okay, Salute... cool story...isn't this chapter about interviews?

Why, yes, young scholar...it is, in fact, about interviewing.

After our first meeting, Ryan scheduled plenty of mock interviews with me prior to his plethora of formal and informal/informational interviews with other organizations. We rehearsed question after question, went over portfolios, previous experience, clubs, activities, GPA, etc. He asked, "Well, what if they don't ask me these questions?"

"Tell your story," I'd say.

The reason that you practice questions is not for you to nail those exact questions. The reasons are a few fold:

1. It's VERY challenging talking about yourself. Like…seriously. Start a conversation right now by telling someone about yourself and keeping their interest while making it relevant. "Tell me about yourself" is, quite frankly, the hardest question to answer. It's not a verb. It's not a noun. It's not a trait or a feeling. It's intangible and almost impossible to answer. And you can definitely say the wrong things if you haven't figured out which stories not to tell.

2. The back and forth of rapport is hard to fake. Being your genuine self under pressure actually does take practice. We often think we're being genuine when we're being hokey or dramatically attentive. Those are very easy to see through and awfully damaging to your professional reputation, as well as your confidence. Trying so hard at the wrong technique is like punching with your arm and not your hips. You expend all of your energy and don't make an impact.

3. Things like posture, where to put your hands, how to fold your legs, etc. can be rehearsed. There are manipulative tactics like "mirroring" that I don't endorse. But I do endorse flow and positive body language. Breathing, over-speaking, pauses that are too long, etc. All of that can give your interviewer a bad impression.

Caldwell went through a series of interviews with:

- Me
- Our incredible alumni connector and his network of alums
- Finally, a former student of mine who worked at one of the major three investment banks in the world.

The reaction from this last interviewer was exactly what a mentor would expect.

"Wow…" he said. "What a humble and capable guy. We're going to find a spot for him." He commented specifically on Caldwell's genuineness, intelligence, and ability to talk to people about the world of finance and investments. He even told me things that I didn't know about Caldwell. Things that just come out naturally when two folks are talking and learning about one another. It was a very proud moment.

Caldwell wound up being offered a position there upon graduation and has been there ever since. We stay in touch, and I believe he's building a pretty solid business for himself. He is climbing the ladder, building internal networks, and learning to grow his own professionalism into a solid career path.

Caldwell had natural ability: intelligence, ability to carry a conversation, analytic sense. He had an upbringing that allowed him access to wealth, adult conversations and culture. And, trust me, in today's 2021, I am not about to say that those things are not important legs up in the race.

But what set Caldwell apart was his ability to use everything he knew about himself, the industry he wanted to work in, the demographic they approached, the company he was interviewing with, and how he would fit into that atmosphere. And his mindset of humility, respect and ambition forced him to interview and prepare until he was able to communicate those things in a high-stakes environment, which is completely different from discussing it over dinner with your family or in your professor's office.

Interviewing has a lot to do with your story. It also has to do with how you tell your story. People with entirely different pasts can have similar successes in their future. Caldwell grew up in wealth and had tons of opportunities for mentorship before his first job. There are others who don't have that experience and don't have the benefit of this book.

What does that equate to? Sometimes you know you want something more and sometimes you know you just want…something. Nobody exemplifies drive more than my brother, Carmine Salute. Yes, I am cheating and using my brother's story in my book. You've already bought it…so read on.

Carmine began his college career like many do, selecting a university that gave him a good gut feeling. And, to be honest…that's the majority of what I hope you get from this book…go with your gut in many instances. Unfortunately, Carmine's gut feeling cannot be replicated, so I'll try to exemplify a few of his decisions to help you make yours.

I remember when Carmine first entered his freshman year at a large state university close to home. He stayed in the dorms because he was an athlete. By the end of the first semester, Carmine had realized he'd made the wrong choice. As with many college athletes (and let's be honest, college students), he was led to believe the college experience he signed up for would be much different than it actually was. This is fairly common. I remember speaking to a student once and telling him he would be absolutely perfect for our Global Studies program, where a student visits about 15 countries. He gave me every indication that that program was the right one for him; I don't say something like that lightly. His reply, after a few meetings, was that his local state school had one of the best study-abroad programs in the country. I googled them. I hadn't heard of them, and their study-abroad program wasn't ranked anywhere. A recruiter definitely said something like "Oh, our study-abroad program? It's the best. In my opinion, it's the best in the country." A 16-year-old hears that and makes a decision. End of story.

After Carmine took some time to evaluate what he wanted, he finished his Associate's Degree at our local community college (A. Never knock a community college for various reasons and B. Ours was ranked in the top 3 of the country, consecutively, year after year). Sometimes a community college is a great idea for those who want to stay home and save money, especially if they are not sure of the direction of their degree career. Are you going to find advanced engineering classes at a community college? Absolutely not. But you can get an Associate's Degree in Business, lots of liberal arts programs, etc. Taking two years to establish yourself, your career, your study habits, and your academics, while finding the right school for you is a great idea. And should you decide to finish your education at a four-year program, your diploma doesn't have an asterisk next to it. Your degree is listed as-is.

Carmine then became a two-sport athlete at Sacred Heart University. His degree is in Business Administration, with a Minor in Sports Management. (He'll tell you it's still a dream of his to work in sports, even on a smaller scale, after his first career is over.) He lived at home at first and began his first job at a collection agency. He made $12 an hour (this was the early 2000s) plus commission for every collection he made.

"That was my first sales job if you think about it," said Carmine. "I really enjoyed it." He said he learned how to call, speak, set an agenda, negotiate, convince, and persuade. Carmine had acquired that interview through a family connection.

We had a neighbor, Dan McCarthy. I remember seeing him at the bus stop in the mornings before work. He would take a bus to the train, train to the city, and then get to his office at Bloomberg, Inc. Neither my brother nor I had heard of Bloomberg, but Dan was the CFO of this company. Dan asked my brother if he needed a job. My brother replied, "Yeah, sure." The reality was that Carmine knew he wouldn't have a career at the small business he was currently at. But he hadn't a clue what Bloomberg was or that it would set him on a path to success.

Dan told Carmine that he would find an entry-level role in his division that Carmine could apply for, which he did. He set him up on his first interview and Carmine went in.

"I didn't prepare for the initial interview," said Carmine. He suggests that folks take an in-depth look at the website of the company they are applying to. "We couldn't do that back then," he said. "Sites just didn't have that information."

To make matters worse, he and the interviewer clashed. It just wasn't a good experience. So he wasn't asked back for a second interview. Dan helped him find some better fits and he interviewed again.

"This time, I prepped better," said Carmine. He had a good rapport with the interviewer, went in about three or four times to meet with different folks, and ultimately, met with the head of recruiting. You're going to love his answer to the next question that was asked of him:

"Why do you want the job?"
"Because I need money."

Carmine said the interviewer noted that the answer resonated with them because it was true.

"They'll find out if you weren't honest," says Carmine. "Always be honest because you'll find a better fit," he says.

"Nowadays," Carmine goes on, "There's more to it. "Even interns are asked to sell a product on the spot so they can sell."

Carmine began in accounts payable, which makes sense as a family friend of the CFO. It took Carmine a little while to realize he liked the company but hated his role in accounts payable. Bloomberg is pretty awesome in that they do allow internal movement pretty frequently. He went into various departments that were sales-like. Eventually, Carmine left Bloomberg very well trained, which does tend to happen with large companies who have stellar training. Smaller firms can find those candidates easily.

"There's an attractiveness to Bloomberg salespeople," said Carmine. "The training is well done and they know their stuff."

So Carmine started at a smaller firm called Valueline. There at a smaller firm, he learned a more grassroots sales approach: prospecting for his own leads, cold calling, qualifying, etc.

"...convince them to buy what I'm selling versus taking orders for a product that was well known in the market [Bloomberg]. But, it was agony." - Carmine Salute

Carmine moved to companies like Thomson Reuters and landed at MarkIt. As a risk-averse human, Carmine decided to make a gut decision and apply for a role in a new product that had no sales team.

One tip he learned from the recruiter who prepared him? "Interview them, don't just get interviewed." - Recruiter

Carmine prepped well, knowing that he was an asset to the firm. He and a small team took a product that nobody was working on and turned it into his career. He is now a Vice President of a 700 person division.

I always like to share mistakes from successful folks in my books and in my class (it'll actually be the theme of my next book). Carmine cited one of his biggest mistakes as hastily taking one of two jobs he was once up for. He'd interviewed at two different firms when he was looking for a big move towards the beginning of his career. He'd been doing well in sales and wanted to run a division. So his second choice firm offered him a job first. It was a fine position, but not his number one pick.

Carmine took the position and put in his two weeks' notice. In the interim, his top pick called him and offered him the job he really wanted. What a predicament to be in! We call those "high-class problems" or "high-class decisions." Carmine asked his new firm for an employment contract, and it took a few days to process. At the time, Carmine had a two-week-old child (my niece, Chloe). He wasn't going to lose an opportunity with Choice #2 in the hopes that the contract would come in, as he liked.

So, on the advice of his top choice HR firm (and his own instinct kicked in, as well), he started his new job. Four. Days. Later...he got the contract he wanted and had to quit a second job in a two-week span. The managing director who hired him was initially ticked but understood Carmine's position. They re-emptied the office and hired again.

"We actually kept in touch, and he became a great contact for me at my new job."

I could honestly write another 15 pages on the interview I had with my brother, Carmine. This book is full of my personal feelings and thoughts. This chapter is no different. I have always been impressed with my brother, but his professionalism during this process and the stories he told really brought that view to full fruition. Since I can't write another 15 pages, I will leave you with this bit of information on how he searches for and hires an intern.

"Now, it's different," says Carmine. "They do interview prep, sales courses. If those things were allotted to me, I wasn't paying attention."

Carmine looks for traits that he would have in himself. Did the candidate create an agenda? Ask him questions? Keep him engaged? He's looking for a fit more than skills.

If you get the job and quit, it's a real pain..." says Carmine. "I wish I could just ask 'Can you do the job?' because that would be much easier." Further, "If they aren't running an interview the way I would run it, it's not a good fit. Have conviction," he says. "Ask difficult questions."

For entry-level candidates or interns, Carmine looks for folks who can get to the point. But that's just part of the equation. "We're trying to change the narrative in our hiring practices," he says. The stereotypical "white male" from 20 or 30 years ago cannot fill their offices. They have always taken diversity into account, as a more diverse workforce, he says, is scientifically proven to create more and better ideas, which means profitability. But there are more valuable reasons, he says, now. It's important to really create a diverse workforce to change that stereotype and provide more opportunities.

Carmine Salute earned his Bachelor's Degree in Business Administration, with a minor in Sports Management. He says it's still a dream to work in sports, one day, but in a light-hearted tone.

PROFESSOR'S PRO TIP

Carmine and Ryan are both two of the most charismatic people I know, both for different reasons. Ryan's ability to talk to anyone makes him an incredible asset. Carmine's uncanny ability to be straight with you means that when he sells you something, he believes in it. But there's one major reason that Ryan scored his job faster than Carmine: preparation. They both had solid networks. Ryan, who graduated nearly 20 years later, had better mentors earlier on who helped him prepare for what needed to be done. This includes, but is not limited to, multiple mock interviews, reading through company websites thoroughly,

KNOWING YOURSELF WELL, and knowing what your strengths are and what story you want to tell.

That's an important factor: telling your story. When I mock interviewed Ryan, I first asked him, "What stories will you tell about yourself that will prove yourself an asset to the company?" His reply was normal.

"It'll depend on the questions I am asked, right?"

"Absolutely not, I replied." He looked confused, rightfully so.

"Ryan, I don't care what is asked of you. If you want to tell a story of resilience about how you won a championship swim meet in high school, you tell that story. Someone asks, 'Tell me about a time when you were a leader…' you tell that story. Someone asks, 'Can you tell me about a time when you were resilient?' You tell that story. If someone asks what your work style is and you want to say that you are ambitious, strong, and love a challenge….you tell that story. Savvy?"

Bottom line: there are multiple stories about your work style, work ethic, leadership skills, etc. you should have prepared. That story has multiple layers and elements, does it not? Therefore, you should have lots of opportunities to tell that story. You can totally tell your story when given the opportunity. Don't force it, it'll happen.

FROM THE EXPERTS

1. 18 percent of social media users can't go beyond "a few hours" without checking Facebook, and 61 percent of users check their newsfeed "at least once a day." - As reported by Inc.com, a report by TotalDUI (a non-profit out of the University of Maryland). The same article discussed the emergence of "Social Media Rehab" programs. These programs have risen in popularity, consistently, since 2016.

2. More than 70 percent of people land jobs through actual networking. - US News estimates. On the other side of that report, it was found that 85 percent of most firms' roles were not filled by online postings.

3. Only 11% of LinkedIn users have more than 100 people in their network - Hubspot, 2017

What's the moral of the story? Build a small online presence; have some fun. But genuine face-to-face connections are part of an art we all need to do a better job at mastering.

Use the following chart to track your interviews and follow-ups, as necessary.

Organization	Website	Interview Date	Interview Time	Interviewer	Research Notes	Post Interview Notes	Follow Up Email Sent

AFTERWORD

Well, there you have it: The College Admission. The bottom line is that nobody has all of the answers. And you may ultimately decide that the four-year traditional institute is not for you. There are SO many choices you have to make. Now, remember the choices that universities make about you. Remember how the university system began:

When folks like Aristotle and Socrates were teaching and learning, and well into history just a few centuries ago, a group of students would get together and ask for learning. In fact, as the movement progressed, they'd pool their money and hire that professor.

Now, we as universities interview and "hire" you to spend your money with us. But forget the curtains and bells and whistles. Remember that we need you to be successful. A note from Greg Wagner, Enrollment Expert:

Every school, whether large or small, that admits a student, wants to turn that student from an admit to a commit. One reason is completely anathema to the "focus on the individual" they all promote; it raises their national ranking when they have a high yield — the number of students who enroll divided by the number who were accepted equals a college's yield rate — and makes them look highly desirable. However, large schools and small schools, while seeking high yield, go about it differently.

The large school is interested in numbers, think of it as a machine churning through tens of thousands of applications and bits of data toward thresholds; those accepted get a shiny package full of promises, and those that don't, well, we know what they get—rejected. The small school has the luxury of taking more time to sift through their applications, look for legacies, and the student with the potential for a good fit.

Small schools can balance their incoming Freshman class if they see a pattern they want to correct, say for example they have a group of athletes from the east coast, they begin to seek musicians or artists from the west coast. They can also fill half their incoming class with "early admits," and then cherry-pick the best students for the other half. But being smart doesn't guarantee admission; admission counselors are less reliant on standardized tests and see some grade inflation in GPAs.

All schools, however, struggling to fill their enrollment goals rely on "designated interest," a component of the admissions process that allows schools to make the best guess possible for those they admit. How do you demonstrate designated interest? Physically visit the school that most interests you, email their admissions counselor that is assigned to your territory, establish a relationship with that person (that's their job!), attend information sessions. join their Facebook or social media page, (yes, they look!). These help paint a picture and can make a break an application to a school of any size.

ABOUT THE AUTHOR

Christopher Salute is both a digital marketing and human development expert with experience ranging from KBC Bank to Yahoo! Inc. to Clearchannel Broadcasting. He began his career in internet sales for a small broadcast equipment company on Long Island and parlayed this experience into his love for broadcasting and internet business. At an early age, Salute set up and managed New York offices to buy and sell broadcast and professional audio equipment. He then moved into finance, where he helped launch an internet platform for ad sales within a proprietary lead generation software. After working at Yahoo! Inc., Salute managed over 30 websites and consulted for over 100 small internet businesses. He spent the rest of his corporate career in luxury brands and startups, helping create internet presences for high end beauty products in manufacturing, marketing, and business development as well as startups in the human capital space.

Salute has spent the last 10 years in academia as a non-traditional Dean/Asst. Dean… rebranding and recruiting for small Universities through new programs and inclusion, including Molloy College, Mercy College, Long Island University, and Sierra Nevada University. He's also taught and advised at countless others. Salute has spoken and advised students on 4 continents and helped thousands of students select the right path for them. He also owns and operates the largest plus size media brand in the world, which includes Bold Magazine, fabUplus Magazine, and Strutter Magazine.

Salute has a dog named Joker and enjoys writing, spoken word poetry, playing guitar, fighting MMA, and cooking. He lives in Las Vegas, NV and loves his family.

www.ingramcontent.com/pod-product-compliance
Lightning Source LLC
Chambersburg PA
CBHW071849070526
44583CB00016B/1613